D0375049

THE TAO OF COACHING

THE TAO OF COACHING

BOOST YOUR EFFECTIVENESS AT WORK BY INSPIRING AND DEVELOPING THOSE AROUND YOU

Max Landsberg

HarperCollins*Publishers*
77–85 Fulham Palace Road,
Hammersmith, London W6 8JB

Published by HarperCollins*Publishers* 1996
9 8 7 6 5 4 3 2 1

Max Landsberg asserts the moral right to
be identified as the author of this work

A catalogue record for this book is
available from the British Library

ISBN 0 00 255784 3

Set in Garamond

Printed and bound by
Caledonian International Book Manufacturing Ltd, Glasgow

*To my parents, who remain
excellent coaches*

Contents

Introduction: Coaching – a Vital Skill for Leaders

Introduction:
Coaching – a Vital Skill
for Leaders

Would you like to:

- Create more time for yourself?
- Develop a band of colleagues who relish working with you?
- Benefit from greater effectiveness, both among those who work for you and in your organisation more broadly?
- Build stronger skills in coaching, which you can apply both at work and beyond?

If so, you are not alone. You are one of a new breed of leaders – a breed which recognises that autocracy no longer works, yet that 'empowerment' alone is not enough. This new breed aspires to influence people and events by adopting the age-old skills of coaching. These skills were known to great masters and their apprentices of old, were lost in the dark ages of society's industrialisation, but have lately been rediscovered by more effective organisations and teams.

The complexity inherent in today's business environment means that the autocrat is no longer in a position to make better decisions than 'subordinates' are able to make collectively, can no longer be sufficiently omniscient to monitor everything, nor omnipresent enough to take all corrective actions needed. Yet, at the opposite extreme, the effectiveness of the purely 'empowering' manager has not been proven.

So the new breed of manager employs a broader repertoire of management styles – sometimes 'hands-on', sometimes 'hands-off', as suits the occasion. But s/he also makes extensive use of the coaching techniques illustrated in this book.

Figure 1

THE TAO OF COACHING

Increase your effectiveness as a leader

Help others to develop and grow

Typical beliefs of great coaches:

You can't be a leader without a following
The autocratic boss is facing extinction
Investing ten minutes in coaching will save an hour
How to win friends and influence people – become a great coach

---

Note: See Tao *in the Glossary*

More practically, this new breed recognises that 'even the master cannot do the whole job unaided'; that the master-leader therefore has to delegate appropriately; that a following of able apprentices is a must for the truly effective leader; and that it is often the leader her/himself who is best placed to build the abilities, on the job, of colleagues.

The creed of the new-style leader includes the beliefs that investing ten minutes in coaching an apprentice will eventually save the master an hour; and that the twin notions of (1) helping others to develop and grow, and (2) increasing your effectiveness as a leader are simply two sides of the same coin (Figure 1).

This book aims to guide you towards becoming an expert coach.

Coaching

So, what do we mean by coaching? **Coaching aims to enhance the performance and learning ability of others. It involves providing feedback, but it also uses other techniques such as motivation, effective questioning and consciously matching your management style to the coachee's readiness to undertake a particular task. It is based on helping the coachee to help her/himself through dynamic interaction – it does not rely on a one-way flow of telling and instructing.**

A glance at the contents page and the glossary will show you the basic toolkit of the great coach. And, after reading the nearly true story in the following brief chapters, you should be able to practise applying it.

The good news is that becoming an effective coach requires only that you develop some simple habits and build one or two basic interpersonal skills. With the inclination, and some practice, most people can become truly *memorable* coaches.

This book

The best way to pick up these habits and skills, of course, is to work with one or more people who are already great coaches. You will see them in action, and see at first hand the benefits – both to themselves and to others – of what they do. These habits would sound simple in a lecture, but their true power only becomes apparent in a real-life setting.

As the next best thing to supplying such a real-life role model, this book aims to be a 'pocket coach' by providing a linked set of parables drawn from the work-life of an almost real person. It follows his career as he coaches, and is coached, both well and badly. Each chapter ends with a summary of the key lessons, and suggestions for how to practise the illustrated habits and skills.

To use this guide most effectively, you might want to:

1. Skim through the story, identifying the situations or ideas which are most relevant to you now.

2. Complete a quick self-appraisal (Appendix 1, page 106). It will only take you a minute to complete, and will provide real sign-posts to topics on which you could usefully work. Also ask people with whom you work to complete a copy of this form based on their impressions of you.

3. Pick a topic to practise this week – perhaps it's 'feedback', perhaps it's 'asking questions instead of telling'. Practise other topics when they appear most relevant and valuable to you.

4. Reappraise yourself after a month, or ensure you elicit some 'up-ward feedback' (see Chapter 3 – *Eliciting Feedback*).

* * *

In today's business environment, the successful manager needs to be as adept at 'soft' skills, like coaching, as s/he is at, 'hard' skills, like finance and strategy. As Lee Iaccoca said, 'Inventories can be man-aged, but people need to be led'.

Of course there *are* situations in which coaching is inappropriate, where decisive or emergency action is called for. Consequently, this guide is intended to help you identify both where – and how – you can use coaching techniques for the direct benefits of yourself and others.

Max Landsberg
London
April 1996

1. Contemplating Coaching at Work

In which Alex examines whether his skills as a coach warrant his being elected to the Board

Alex wondered whether this was his last chance. Although he had been promoted into a senior management position, it had taken a year longer than he had expected. The question now was whether he would be elected to the Board of Directors – and what would happen to him if he failed. It was now or never, and it wouldn't be plain sailing. 'At least,' he thought, 'I've given it my best shot. I might as well enjoy my vacation.'

Alex settled back into his chair beside the pool and gazed out over the Aegean, oblivious to the playful shrieks from the beach below. He tried to relax, but wished he'd arranged the vacation for two weeks later, after the Board back in London had made its decision.

He congratulated himself, however, on having rented a villa with one of the few telephones on the island which actually worked. Perhaps he'd get a call after the Board meeting? He glanced nervously over his shoulder to check that no-one had accidentally left the phone off the hook, unplugged it, or otherwise reduced it to the normal state of telephones on the island.

As if by telepathy, the phone rang. Was it for Alex? It was! Was it his secretary Julia back at the office? It was! Was he now a Director? 'I'm afraid they've had to delay the meeting until tomorrow – I thought I should let you know,' she apologised.

'No problem,' he said, cursing inaudibly. 'I'll speak to you again soon.'

* * *

1

He thought about last week's day trip to Delphi. What were the words carved above the gateway to the Oracle's chair, to prepare the ancient enquirers on their way to the prophet? That's it: 'Know thyself!'

'OK,' he resolved, 'half an hour of introspection, my own decision on whether I deserve to be a Director, and then unadulterated vacation.'

* * *

The problem was in some senses straightforward. Alex knew that, on the plus side, he had led a major reorganisation, implemented a courageous acquisition and turned around a loss-making subsidiary. The only minus – but it had been a major one – was that he had on occasion tended to use people, and burnt them out. He had acquired a reputation as a 'people-eater'; at one point it had reached a stage where no-one really wanted to work for him, or with him.

Five years earlier, the Board might have overlooked this character flaw. But now the management skills and habits necessary for building people's abilities, for helping them to develop, for coaching them, had assumed far greater importance. A deficiency in this area would not go unnoticed.

Deep down, Alex knew that this new emphasis on people development had been driven by several powerful forces which were now affecting most large companies. First had been a trend towards reducing the number of management levels in organisations' hierarchies – i.e., 'delayering'. Everyone was now working in cross-functional teams for large proportions of their time. No longer were jobs and roles prescribed and static, so no longer could 'bosses' just go on telling 'subordinates' exactly what to do. Rather, the successful companies were now those in which people learnt new skills and habits from each other, and in which managers were also coaches.

Second, labour markets had changed. The most able people now knew that companies with a coaching culture did exist, and that it was much more fun and rewarding to work there. In addition, people were more mobile, and excellent organisations were focusing more on bringing out their people's potential in order to retain their best performers.

Third, business conditions, markets and technologies were now changing even more rapidly than in the past. This meant that companies could no longer rely on providing employees with a week or two of 'off-site training courses' every year. Training now had to be continuous and 'on the job' – i.e., by coaching.

'Well,' mused Alex, 'am I good enough at this coaching stuff?' Intuitively he thought he was indeed now a good coach. He hadn't been a 'natural' at it when he had joined the company a few years ago, but he'd picked up a few good coaching habits along the way. These had helped him to become much more effective as a manager, so he had kept an eye open for more tips from coaches who were role models. He had also read a great book on the subject, and had put into practice many of its suggestions. His only problem had come about a year ago when pressures to achieve had caused him to slip back into some bad old habits, resulting in his failure to be elected a Director.

But he had decided to mend his ways, and people now wanted to work with him again. He even found that his personal relationships outside work had improved.

* * *

On balance, he was about to elect himself a Director . . . To be absolutely certain of his decision, however, he decided to review his own 'moments of truth' in coaching during his time with the company. This would allow him to reach a well-informed decision. It would also provide the basis for lending his weight to the company-wide coaching programme – his avowed mission if he was indeed promoted to the Board.

With the benefit of hindsight, Alex began to review how much he'd learnt about coaching – not only from his own coaching practices as a senior manager, but also from his early experiences of having been coached by others.

He picked up his hand-held dictating machine and began to speak, recalling the lessons of his career since he'd first joined the company.

This is Alex's story . . .

'Ludwig, are you deaf or what? If I've told you once, I've told you a thousand, times, drop the *music schoozic* and get a proper job . . .'

2. Asking Versus Telling

In which Alex learns that 'coaching by asking' is often more effective than 'coaching by telling'

Alex was tearing his hair out. He had just joined the company as a manager of strategic planning, and was halfway through his first project. He was used to gathering facts on market trends, and analysing lots of numbers, but he wasn't used to writing the succinct reports that seemed to be the norm in this, his new company. He had developed what he thought was a creative title page for his document: 'Acquisition in the ice-cream market – cold logic or soft option?' But he was having real problems in structuring his thoughts for the main body of the report.

He took a deep breath and set off down the corridor to find Bob, his boss. 'You need to start with the main message,' Bob explained, 'and then structure the supporting rationale – ideally into three points, because most audiences can easily assimilate three points – in one of two ways. Either use a grouping of parallel points, or use a logical flow of argument: statement, implication, resolution. I have to go to a meeting now, but let's meet up later to run through your draft.' Alex had been confused by this rapid set of instructions which hadn't made immediate sense to him, and by the end of the afternoon had not made much progress.

Alex wondered whether Sarah could help. As a senior marketing manager, she had been involved in recruiting Alex into the company, and he suspected that she had been influential in the decision to offer him the job. She and Alex had many things in common – they had both been to the same business school, they were both interested in direct marketing, and they were both accomplished tennis players.

Sarah was sympathetic to Alex's plight in structuring the report. 'What's the most extreme statement you would feel comfortable making about this ice-cream market?' she asked.

'Well, I'm not yet sure that we should actually enter the market, but it does look attractive,' he replied.

'And why does it look attractive?'

'Well, demand is rising, profit margins look sustainable, competition does not seem to be very intense, and prices have held up over the last five years.'

'I see,' she replied, 'and are any of these four points really different sides of the same coin?'

'I guess the point about pricing is really part of the statement about profit margins . . . Hey . . .,' he continued excitedly, 'I think I've got something on costs, too. So, I could say that the market is attractive because: (1) demand is rising; (2) profit margins are sustainable on both the price and cost side; and (3) competitors look likely to remain weak.

'Thanks, Sarah. I think I can work on this structure. By the way, is this a grouping of reasons or a flow of argument? It looks like a grouping of reasons to me . . .'

* * *

Alex was impressed by Sarah's approach. By spending just four minutes with him, instead of Bob's two minutes, she had really helped him with structuring the report – and she didn't even know anything about the ice-cream market! She had just asked the right questions. He also felt more confident about drafting the next report, and thought he'd probably be able to learn a lot from working with Sarah in the future, if the opportunity arose.

Sarah, too, thought that the brief interaction had been worthwhile; she believed that Alex had a lot of raw talent, and hoped to co-opt him to work on one of her projects in the future.

The Coaching Spectrum

Socrates saw himself as a 'midwife to understanding'. He believed that one could *help* people understand, but that one could not *make* people understand – just as a midwife delivers, but does not give birth to, the child.

Similarly, the coach is a 'midwife to skill building', not typically a highly didactic teacher. And the coach's most important decision is whether to issue an instruction or to ask a question – or to use a style of interaction somewhere between these two extremes. You will face this decision in a wide variety of coaching situations – when deciding the topic on which to help the coachee, when providing feedback or when helping the coachee decide what to do next.

At work, many 'bosses' rely on *telling* others – directly or indirectly – what to do and (sometimes) how to do it. But, as a coach, it's important to have a broader range of approaches in your repertoire. Often, the *pivotal question* is more powerful than the instruction, as Socrates knew.

If there is one thing you do differently as a result of reading this book, it should be simply to try asking a few good questions where you might otherwise have issued an instruction or leapt into providing advice, as illustrated by Alex's story on the preceding pages.

The Ask/Tell Repertoire

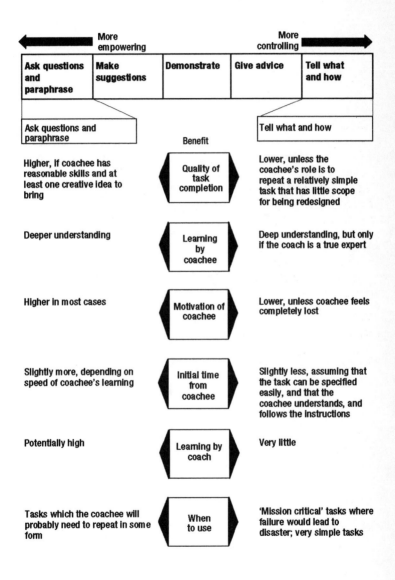

More empowering ← → More controlling

Ask questions and paraphrase	Make suggestions	Demonstrate	Give advice	Tell what and how

Ask questions and paraphrase | **Benefit** | **Tell what and how**

Ask questions and paraphrase	Benefit	Tell what and how
Higher, if coachee has reasonable skills and at least one creative idea to bring	Quality of task completion	Lower, unless the coachee's role is to repeat a relatively simple task that has little scope for being redesigned
Deeper understanding	Learning by coachee	Deep understanding, but only if the coach is a true expert
Higher in most cases	Motivation of coachee	Lower, unless coachee feels completely lost
Slightly more, depending on speed of coachee's learning	Initial time from coachee	Slightly less, assuming that the task can be specified easily, and that the coachee understands, and follows the instructions
Potentially high	Learning by coach	Very little
Tasks which the coachee will probably need to repeat in some form	When to use	'Mission critical' tasks where failure would lead to disaster; very simple tasks

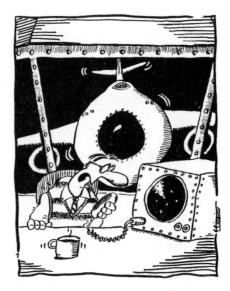

'Oh, is that so. Well I'm the Top Banana, Head Honcho, Big Cheese, around here matey, and I say you're at thirty thousand feet!'

Key point: Receiving feedback *does* involve listening actively

3. Eliciting Feedback

In which Alex learns how to elicit feedback from a colleague

Six months into his career with the company, Alex was feeling satisfied with his progress. He thought he understood how the company operated, and he had already made some substantial contributions. Although he didn't yet manage anyone else, he had practised his 'effective questioning' technique to good effect. On more than one occasion, he had constructively changed the course of a meeting through a well-planted question – even though he already knew the answer.

But one thing still puzzled him. 'How on earth do I find out how well I'm doing? No-one *ever* seems to tell me directly.'

The ice-cream project had been moved to the back burner – a move which Alex thought had obvious dangers! – and Alex was now working with Bob, his boss, on a project to streamline the company's production processes. He had been looking forward to the project, since he thought he had some particularly relevant skills to contribute. After all, he had studied engineering at university and had then worked as a production manager for two years before going to business school.

The project had started well. Alex had developed a good working relationship with Bob and felt that his work so far had been of real value. He had even had his first opportunity to make a full presentation to the divisional board.

However, he realised that he was not getting much coaching or feedback. He had broached the subject tentatively with Bob a few times, including immediately after the last presentation. But Bob had merely responded that Alex seemed to be doing very well – and was, in fact, exceeding Bob's expectations.

Alex decided to seek Sarah's advice, and took the opportunity to sit next to her at lunch in the canteen. 'Sarah, I can't seem to get Bob to tell me properly how I'm performing. How do *you* manage to elicit helpful and constructive feedback?'

Her response was disarmingly simple. 'You have to ask, and you have to listen.'

* * *

Several days later, Alex tried it out. 'Bob, could we have half an hour together, so that you could give me some feedback on how I've been doing for the last couple of months?'

'OK, Alex, but what would you like feedback on? I'm a bit surprised that you're asking for feedback, because I didn't really think that you wanted any.'

'What made you think that?' quizzed an astonished Alex.

'Well, you didn't take the initiative to talk through with me, when we started the project, the areas in which you wanted to build your skills. Also, the one time I did try to give you some feedback, you seemed very defensive.'

Alex did not want to become confrontational, but he did point out his two subsequent attempts to discuss his performance.

'Yes, I remember,' Bob replied, 'but both requests were in front of several other people. I got the impression that you were merely seeking public acclaim. That said, I'm sorry for not following up later on. Anyway, on what specific area would you like to have my feedback?'

Alex was unsure. He had assumed that Bob, with his greater experience, would know exactly what to focus on. However, they agreed to meet the next day, after Alex had thought about the areas in which he would most value some help.

They focused on Alex's strengths and weaknesses in delivering presentations, and had a highly productive half hour. Bob helped Alex to realise that he needed to establish eye contact with each person in the audience instead of with only one person, and that he needed to set the context more clearly at the beginning of his presentation.

As Alex left Bob's office he really did feel 'coached' – rather than 'evaluated'; Bob had been careful to discuss specific examples of what Alex had done, rather than talking about character 'traits'. Alex also had a clear plan of action.

'I suppose that obtaining feedback is as easy as "ask and listen",' thought Alex, 'although both you and your coach need to know enough about you to address the right topics, and you have to be careful to listen with an open mind, and without being defensive.'

* * *

Alex had jotted down the points on the following two pages for future reference, and had found them as helpful later on – when he had become a more senior manager – as they had been on that day. He also recalled a fragment of a poem which he had learnt by heart as a schoolboy:

> *If you can trust yourself when all men doubt you,*
> *But make allowance for their doubting too . . .*
> Rudyard Kipling

Getting Feedback

When was the last time that you received useful feedback? Probably too long ago: few people ever feel that they receive enough feedback. This is true for older as well as for younger people. For the experienced as well as for the inexperienced. For the able as well as for the less able.

Although the primary focus of this book is on how to be a great coach, it is worth touching on the skill of being a great *coachee*. It's a valuable skill for the workplace, as well as for life in general. Managers who fail to *receive* feedback (for whatever reason) disable an important self-correcting mechanism and aid to personal productivity.

However, you cannot be a furtive coachee – you have to make it clear that you want feedback. In addition, in asking for feedback you are asking someone to do you a favour (one that requires some courage on the coach's part), so you should also make the process as easy as possible for her/him. The facing page provides some suggestions.

1. *Choose the right 'coach' for the right topic, a coach whom you really trust. For example, you might want to choose different peers/subordinates/bosses/ friends, depending on whether you feel you need feedback on:*
   - Management style (choose someone whom you manage)
   - Presentation skills (alert a member of your audience)

2. *Give your coach as much notice as possible, so that s/he can marshal relevant examples*
   - Explain at the beginning of major pieces of work what you would like – e.g., feedback topics and the frequency of discussion
   - Remind your coach prior to the meeting – don't just 'turn up'

3. *Take the initiative in building a trusting relationship*
   - Volunteer your own perspective on areas in which you could improve (don't just try to highlight areas in which you are phenomenally excellent)
   - Explain what motivates you and what demotivates you; disclose other factors that might be relevant

4. *Receive the feedback genuinely*
   - Avoid being defensive (unless you never want feedback again!)
   - Follow what the coach says – show your genuine interest, summarise what you are learning, and ask for specific examples and explanations

5. *Show your appreciation*
   - Make real progress, and follow at least some of the advice
   - Let the coach know that s/he has made a difference; thank the coach

Exercise
- Identify two people from whom you would value feedback this week, and ask for it.

'So just to re-cap, I like to be rubbed here, stroked there and massaged here, but don't ever fidget with this bit . . .'

Key point: Coaching can also benefit the coach

4. Correcting Common Coaching Myths

In which Alex reviews myths about coaching,
and comes to understand the selfish reasons for
becoming a great coach

It had been three weeks since Alex had seen Sarah in the canteen, and he decided to drop by her office. 'Hi, Alex, I haven't seen you for a while, how are you?'

'Fine thanks,' he replied. 'By the way, thanks for your advice on obtaining feedback. I had a really useful session with Bob.'

'That's great,' said Sarah, 'and I'm glad you dropped by, because I was wondering if *you* could do *me* a favour. As you may know, the company's Human Resources Committee is taking a real interest in coaching. As part of the overall project, I thought we should have an article on the topic in the company magazine. Perhaps a few key hints on how to do it, plus a section on why to do it. I've drafted a few pages, and I was hoping you'd be willing to review them and let me have your reaction.'

'I'd be happy to,' he replied, with a slightly confused expression. 'But isn't it fairly straightforward? I mean, don't people just provide feed-back and coaching to help other people get better at their work?'

For the first time, Sarah looked at him condescendingly. 'Well, Alex, there's slightly more to it than that. In fact, the great coach has as many selfish reasons as philanthropic ones to invest a few minutes a day in deploying his or her skills in this area. Anyway, if you have a moment to read through my draft, I'd be very grateful.'

'*The Myths of Coaching* – seems like a good title,' he mumbled, as he left Sarah's office with the draft document.

The Myths of Coaching

Let's face it, coaching is not about being a 'nice guy'. It's about bringing the same structure and creativity to your interactions with colleagues as you bring to solving business problems.

But before we go any further in defining what it takes to be a good coach, let's address head-on some of coaching's myths and realities.

There are five major myths surrounding what it takes to be a good coach. Here's an attempt to set the record straight

by Sarah Jennings

Myth: We coach primarily to help others.
Reality: There are many tangible, selfish and acceptable reasons for one to become a great coach. In fact, good coaches find the personal payoffs so high that they rarely kick the habit. The following – listed in order of decreasing selfishness – is a sample of those payoffs:

- More time for yourself. You can either go home earlier or invest the time in higher quality work. While it's virtually impossible to prove, most great coaches believe that investing just ten minutes a day in coaching team-mates typically generates at least 20 minutes of extra time per day for the coach.

- Better customer relations skills. By coaching colleagues you can hone the interpersonal skills which you need for building effective relations with customers and clients.

- Stronger organisation. If you plan on a long-term career with the company, investing in the development of your colleagues is clearly worthwhile.

- More fun. You and others working in coaching-oriented teams tend to enjoy yourselves more.

- Stronger following. If you help others, they tend to help you. And if you aspire to be a leader, it's worth remembering that every leader needs a following.

> *Coachees can often learn more from a coach asking them how well they've performed a particular task than from being told, 'Here's what you did wrong, and here's what to do next time'*

back is only one tool in the coach's tool box. For example, good coaches typically master the art of effective questioning. Coachees can often learn more from a coach asking 'How well do you think you did; what might you do differently next time?', than from being told, 'Here's what you did wrong, and here's what to do next time'. There are also *other* tools, like the GROW approach and motivation techniques.

Myth: Focus on the coachee.
Reality: Know thyself. Coaches don't focus exclusively on the coachee. In fact, great coaches have a high degree of *self*-awareness. We all have the basic skills to coach; unfortunately, most of us have a few psychological blocks when it comes to applying those skills well and consistently. Great coaches know how to overcome their own blocks.

Myth: Coaching equals feedback.
Reality: There are many other important coaching tools and habits. While most people think that coaching is merely providing feedback and suggestion to coachees, the truth is that insightful feed-

Myth: Coaching requires lots of time.
Reality: The best coaching comes in small doses. Many people believe that coaching comes in large quantums. But with a bit of practice, you don't need to change into a jogging suit every time you want to provide coaching. Small investments of time – as little as five minutes – can yield tangible increases in performance

Myth: Coaching is about work.
Reality: Good coaching will spread to other areas of life. Those who develop their coaching skills at work usually find they are better able to help their friends, partners and children. In that respect, coaching is clearly a *life skill.*

Annual appraisals with Old 'Sparky' Watson tended to be a little traumatic . . .

Key point: Guide – don't judge – when coaching

5. Giving Feedback

In which Alex delivers really effective feedback for the first time

Two weeks later, as Alex was reading Sarah's article on the myths of coaching in the company magazine, he thought about Gordon. Perhaps it was worth investing some time in coaching him.

Gordon, who had just graduated from university and had recently joined the company, was the first person who Alex had had reporting directly to him. The company had renewed its interest in the ice-cream market and Alex, with Gordon's help, had been asked to advise on whether to acquire a large manufacturer of ice cream and frozen yoghurt – Cones-and-Tubs International.

Things had started well: they had assembled the relevant facts, interviewed some of the company's customers, and estimated how much Cones-and-Tubs was worth.

Alex, however, had noticed that Gordon tended to disappear for long periods of time. He was undoubtedly working very hard, because whenever Alex managed to catch up with him, he always had reams of printout from his personal computer, with all sorts of weird and wonderful scenarios analysed in minute detail.

The problem was that Gordon had clearly gone off at a tangent on many occasions, and Alex felt sure this was because he had not really been paying attention in the team meetings which they had held periodically.

'Time for some feedback,' thought Alex, as he flicked through a booklet on giving constructive feedback which Sarah had given him.

The section on delivering feedback started with the usual caveats that there was more to coaching than just giving feedback; that feedback was, however, a critically important tool; and that it was difficult to generalise about how to do it well. 'Nevertheless,' it continued, 'in providing feedback, you should ensure that you address three topics, with the acronym AID to help you remember them:

A (Actions) The things that the coachee is doing well, or poorly, in the area under review

I (Impact) The effect these actions are having

D (Desired outcome) The ways in which the coachee could do things more effectively.

Alex had just closed the booklet when Gordon dropped by for the prearranged meeting. Alex started by reviewing the project's good progress to date, and congratulated Gordon on several aspects of his work so far. Then he continued, 'Gordon, I'd like to give you some feedback on your participation in our team meetings. Would you find that helpful?' Gordon nodded his assent.

'Well, I couldn't help noticing that you sometimes don't appear fully engaged in our team discussions. For example, at the meeting yesterday you seemed to be doodling, and even staring out of the window on occasion. Would you say that was an accurate observation?' *[Description of actions]*

'I do sometimes feel a bit bored by the endless discussions,' Gordon replied. 'I suppose I'd just prefer to be getting on with the analysis.'

'OK, Gordon, but the problem this causes is that when the meeting has finished, and you go off to do your part of the work, you don't take account of changes in direction which everyone else has agreed to at the meeting. As a result, some of your work ends up being redundant, and you come across as rather arrogant, since it appears that you can't be bothered to listen to what your team-mates are saying.' *[Description of impact]*

'I recognise the first point about redundant work, but I didn't realise that I would seem arrogant,' replied Gordon, surprised.

'Let's see what we can do to address the situation,' suggested Alex. 'Do you have any ideas for getting more engaged in these meetings?' *[Discussion of desired outcome]*

Gordon didn't have any immediate ideas; it was, after all, his first 'real' job and he wasn't used to working in teams. So Alex continued, 'How about if we arrange for you to present your most recent work at the beginning of each meeting? Or, better still, why don't we expand your role on the project to include helping me in the overall coordination? That way you would have a reason to keep track of what's going on. Perhaps you could even summarise the agreed next steps at the end of each meeting, before everyone leaves the room.'

* * *

They both thought this was a great idea. As Gordon left the office, Alex reflected that, while this interaction had hardly been substantial or interactive enough to be called 'coaching', it was nevertheless constructive feedback.

Over the next few weeks Gordon became much more engaged in proceedings, his team-mates stopped moaning about him, and Alex found that he could delegate many of the project coordination tasks to Gordon. Alex felt that the AID structure was both simple and effective; he'd try to use it more often in the future.

Providing Feedback

Providing feedback is one of the coach's most important skills. Narrowly defined, it means replaying to the coachee what s/he did in a specific situation. More broadly – and more usefully – defined, it includes highlighting the *impact* of what the coachee did. It also includes a discussion of what the coachee might do (even) better next time.

A few definitions:

- **Positive** feedback applies to situations where the coachee did a good job. It consists of simple praise, but is even more powerfully reinforcing when the coach specifically highlights why or how the coachee did a good job.

- **Constructive** feedback highlights how the coachee could do better next time. It needs to be delivered sensitively.

  - Use the AID mnemonics suggested earlier

  - When describing the coachee's actions, focus on specific observable facts ('In the last presentation you did not fully address some of the follow-up questions'), not assumed traits ('You tend to be evasive')

- **Negative** feedback – i.e., merely replaying something that went wrong – is essentially destructive and is only used, usually by accident, to terminate friendships and marriages. It describes a perceived negative behaviour, without proposing a resolution ('You're always complaining').

To provide a factual context for your discussion of how your coachee performed, you can of course refer to notes which you took at the time, replay a video (if the coachee had agreed to being videoed) or ask a third party to comment.

Helpful Hints for Providing Feedback

Bad feedback	Good feedback	Hallmarks of good feedback
Creates defensiveness and confrontation; focuses on blame	Creates trust and cooperation; focuses on improvements – possible or achieved	• Create a contract to discuss issues • Acknowledge coachee's feelings
Does not improve skill	Increases skill	• Focus on 'skills' not 'person' • Paint specific picture of desired skill • Suggest practical steps
Undermines confidence and self-esteem	Improves confidence in ability and potential	• Position as need to 'build' or 'demonstrate' vs. 'don't have' or 'must prove' • Balance negatives and positives; provide constructive actions
Leaves person guessing	Clarifies 'exactly where I stand' and 'what to do next'	• Verify with questions; ask for coachee's recap • Jointly arrive at plan
Leaves person feeling 'judged'	Leaves person feeling 'helped'	• Invite coachee to assess own performance first • Offer support for future

Exercise
• Identify someone to whom you could provide useful feedback today (see Appendix 2, page 107), and follow through.

As he entered the back straight, Dave faced
seven oncoming speedwalkers and the
dawning realisation that he might have
started off in the wrong direction.

Key point: Organise your coaching
sessions well; start in the correct
direction

6. Structuring the Coaching Session

In which Alex encounters a master coach, and learns how to use the GROW* approach to structure coaching sessions

Alex jumped at the knock on his office door. 'How are you, Alex? I hear that you are developing a reputation for providing useful feedback.'

It was Michael, the Chief Financial Officer of the company. Although he was senior to Alex, he was a part-time member of the multifunctional team – Project Quest – which Alex was leading to advise on the acquisition of Cones-and-Tubs International.

It was only 3 p.m., but Alex looked drained. 'I'm fine, thanks,' he replied without conviction.

'Alex, why not put the work down for half an hour? I can see that something is causing you a problem. Perhaps I can help.'

Alex accepted the offer gratefully. He had a particularly open relationship with Michael, who had been his informal mentor ever since their doubles victory in the company's annual tennis championship. 'I've been with the company for just over a year now, and find that I'm spending a lot of time running meetings. But I can't seem to get the discussions to make as much progress as I'd like. Perhaps I'm doing something wrong.'

'I can spare you 20 minutes,' Michael offered, 'why don't we see if we can figure out something to help you. But first, what is your **goal** –

---

* **G**oal, **R**eality, **O**ptions, **W**rap-up – described on page 31

both regarding the management of meetings in general, and for our next 20 minutes together in particular? In other words, if I could grant you one wish for this session, what would it be?'

'I suppose it would be to have a brief checklist for how to manage meetings better.'

'And do you think we can accomplish that in the next 20 minutes?' Michael enquired.

'Let's give it a go, Michael, there's nothing to lose – I feel a lot better already, even thinking that there might be a solution.'

Michael asked Alex to be more specific about the **reality** of the situation. Just how did Alex know that there really was a problem? Were there particular situations in which he felt more, or less, able to manage the dynamics of meetings? What solutions had he tried so far? Of course, Michael had himself been a participant in many of the meetings which Alex had been chairing, and so was able to offer one or two of his own observations. However, he knew that it was Alex who had to do the diagnosis, if the ideas were to be useful.

Initially, Alex had felt that the main reason for his difficulty was a lack of ability in dealing with several awkward team members. But with Michael's guidance in thinking things through, he also realised that he didn't pay enough attention to planning the meetings in advance. 'So, Alex, which topic would you like to focus on – people or planning?'

'Let's talk about planning the meetings,' replied Alex. 'I'll need to put in some more thought before addressing the issue of how to interact with difficult team members.'

'OK, so let's focus on the **options** you have. What could you try? What have you seen work well in similar circumstances? Try to be radical.'

Alex reflected for a moment. 'I suppose I could put more thought into my preparations for the meeting.'

'How do you mean?' probed Michael, moving to the flipchart.

'Well, currently I prepare an agenda with a simple list of the topics for discussion. In future I could be more focused and actually list the specific issues we need to resolve. I could even list the team's hypotheses for resolving each issue – and circulate it prior to the meeting. That way we could really be focused.' Alex was beginning to look relieved, and he continued to brainstorm other ideas for better meeting preparation, with Michael throwing in occasional ideas of his own. (Michael even made a mental note of some of these ideas for his own subsequent use.)

'Time to **wrap up**,' said Michael, glancing at his watch. 'Do you think you'll actually do any of this? What are the next steps? What support do you need, if any?'

Alex was sure that he would adopt the ideas they had just come up with – they would certainly be helpful. He also felt that he understood himself a little better, and would have more confidence to address similar issues in future. 'The only further favour I would ask, Michael, is that you give me a kick under the table at the next meeting if I haven't done any of the preparation in advance!'

* * *

'Goal, Reality, Options, Wrap-up,' thought Michael, as he was about to leave Alex's office. 'That structure always seems to work if you want to have a really effective coaching session which goes beyond simply providing feedback.'

'By the way, Alex, I really think we'll get approval for this ice-cream acquisition. I've even heard your name mentioned as the person to run the post-merger integration project – and that would probably mean a promotion. Of course, I'd be involved in the project too, as would Sarah Jennings on the marketing side. Do you know Sarah? I think you'd enjoy working with her.'

Structuring a Coaching Session – GROW

So, how do we actually structure a coaching session? The GROW (**G**oal, **R**eality, **O**ptions, **W**rap-up) model is one of the most common coaching tools, widely used by many great coaches.

The framework provides a simple four-step structure for a coaching session. During the first step of a session *[Goal]*, coach and coachee agree on a specific topic and objective for the discussion. During the second step *[Reality]*, both coach and coachee invite self-assessment and offer specific examples to illustrate their points. They then move into the third step *[Options]*, where suggestions are offered and choices made. And finally *[Wrap-up]*, the coach and coachee commit to action, define a timeframe for their objectives and identify how to overcome possible obstacles.

Here are a few tips for using this model:

- Use more 'ask' than 'tell'; elicit useful ideas from your coachee – don't just try to prove you are smart

- Think creatively – not just systematically, particularly in the Options and Wrap-up steps

- Illustrate, and check understanding, throughout by using specific examples – from the coachee's and your own experiences

- If you have a follow-up session, you can obviously lengthen or shorten each of the four steps as needed

- Agree topic for discussion
- Agree specific objective of session
- Set long-term aim if appropriate

- Invite self-assessment
- Offer specific examples of feedback
- Avoid or check assumptions
- Discard irrelevant history

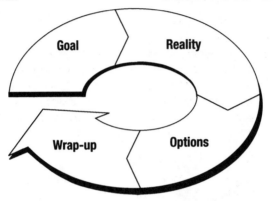

- Commit to action
- Identify possible obstacles
- Make steps specific and define timing
- Agree support

- Cover the full range of options
- Invite suggestions from the coachee
- Offer suggestions carefully
- Ensure choices are made

Exercise
- Find an opportunity to apply GROW this week. See Appendix 3 (page 108) for examples of questions to use.

Thompson and Maguire may not have seen eye to eye but they were the best forensic teams on the Force . . .

Key point: Great teams overcome differences in styles of working

7. Diagnosing Individuals' Different Styles

In which Alex learns how to help two very different people to work together

A couple of weeks later, Alex was beginning to feel that his life was more under control, thanks to Michael's advice on the GROW framework. But he still had problems with Tom and Dick, the two members of the Project Quest team who were always arguing.

Alex was unsure whether to just 'knock their heads together', or whether a more probing approach would have greater and more lasting value. At the end of a meeting with Michael, Alex sought his advice on Tom and Dick. Michael did not beat about the bush.

'I've met them both a few times, Alex. I'll bet you that Tom's an ENFP, and that Dick's an ISTJ.' Alex looked completely blank, so Michael continued, 'Do you know anything about psychology?' Alex shook his head, suddenly thinking that it was a bit absurd that   managers were rarely taught much about what makes people tick.

'Well,' continued Michael, 'luckily, you don't need a degree in psychology to be an effective manager and coach, but you do need some way to figure out the different styles of interaction different people prefer to use.

'Personally, I recommend something called the Myers-Briggs Type Indicator. It sounds a bit of a mouthful, but it's really quite simple. I'll give you a two-minute description, but then I suggest you read a booklet on the subject.

'The Type Indicator provides a description of how people prefer to operate in their daily lives. You know how, in meetings for example, some people like to stick rigidly to the agenda while others prefer to leap from idea to idea? The first type of person could well be an

ISTJ, while the other might be an ENFP. If you know what 'type' a person is, it will help you a good deal in interacting with them – and in helping them to work with each other.

' "So", I hear you ask, "what do these letters stand for?" The Indicator is based on four dimensions of how people prefer to operate. The first dimension relates to how they are *energised* – what turns them on. An Introvert (I) is energised by the inner world of thoughts and ideas, whereas an Extrovert (E) is energised by the outer world of people and things.

'The second dimension describes what the person prefers to pay *attention* to. A Senser (S) focuses on facts and the five senses, while, at the other end of the spectrum, an Intuiter (N) type focuses on what might be, and the sixth sense.

'The third dimension describes how the person prefers to *make decisions*. The Thinker (T) tends to use reason and logic, while the Feeler (F) tends to use values and subjective judgement.

'The final dimension describes the person's *overall approach to life* – with Judgers (J) preferring to be planned and organised, while Perceivers (P) prefer spontaneity and flexibility. If you take all the combinations, you'll find that these dimensions define 16 basic types of person.'

Alex thought he understood. 'So, an ISTJ person [who prefers to be an Introvert and Senser and Thinker and Judger] might think that an ENFP person [Extrovert, Intuiter, Feeler, Perceiver] was lax and disorganised, while the latter would think of the other as unimaginative and afraid of ever taking a leap into the dark? OK, I think I can see how I could use this, but how would I really know someone's "type"?'

'Sounds like an ISTJ kind of question, Alex! You can either have your team complete a standard questionnaire, if you think they're up to sharing the results. Otherwise, you'll just have to use your intuition. Why not have a chat with Tom and Dick separately, with these thoughts in mind, but don't forget to read the caveats in the booklet.'

* * *

Alex set off down the corridor to find Tom. He had always thought that Tom's office was a disorganised mess, but now he understood a little better why this might not bother someone who valued flexibility, creativity and spontaneity.

After his discussions with both Tom and Dick, Alex concluded that the original diagnosis had been correct; far from there being some deep-seated enmity between them, they just had very different preferred styles of working. He knew he had two options: either to reassign Tom and/or Dick to parts of the project in which they would not have to work together, or to address the issue head-on. The latter approach had the advantages that (1) Tom and Dick would not have to get up to speed in new areas of work, and (2) the team could actually be more effective if these two team members could contribute their differing skills in a complementary way.

Alex opted for this latter course. In fact, he had everyone on the team, including himself, complete Type Indicator questionnaires, and share their results. Tom and Dick were wary of each other for a few days, but soon settled down to productive collaboration, based on their better understanding of each other. Not surprisingly, Tom focused on coming up with creative ideas, and Dick on checking their practicality.

However, Alex was surprised to discover that, by the time Project Quest was completed, Tom and Dick had shared their thoughts on what they had consciously learnt from each other. Tom had mapped out the things he could do to be more organised when the occasion required it, and Dick had done likewise for creativity. Alex decided to encourage this type of mutual learning more actively in future.

* * *

Alex reflected on how valuable it was for team members, managers and coaches to have some simple model of how people interact, and to discuss this topic openly. He also realised how many misunderstandings derive from differences in style – rather than the most common interpretation: that the other party is dim-witted or has poor intentions.

'But what's really powerful,' he thought, 'is when you have real insights about individuals' styles, and combine them with the basic tools of coaching – asking effective questions, listening actively, providing clear feedback and using the GROW framework.'

Understanding Preferred Styles

There are many models for identifying and characterising the styles of interaction which we and others prefer to employ. A widely-used approach is the Myers-Briggs Type Indicator (MBTI). It is based on the following four 'dimensions' of a person's preferred approach to life.

1. How you are energised (Extrovert vs. Introvert)

2. What you pay attention to (Sensing vs. Intuition)

3. How you make decisions (Thinking vs. Feeling)

4. How you live and work (Judgement vs. Perception)

To work effectively with someone, take their preferred style into account. For example, 'Judgement' types can become irritated by 'Perception' types who may stray from the agenda. Conversely, people strong on 'Perception' may see those who prefer 'Judgement' as unwilling to take the time to explore creative options.

The characteristics of each dimension are indicated opposite. For a more complete description, see *Please Understand Me* by David Keirsey and Marilyn Bates.

For more information about receiving a profile, contact:

- Oxford Psychologist Press Ltd., Lambourne House, 311 – 321 Banbury Road, Oxford, OX2 7JH, U.K., or
- Consulting Psychologists Press, Inc.,3803 East Bayshore Road, Palo Alto, California 94303, U.S.

(The description of the MBTI has been modified and reproduced by special permission of the Publisher, Consulting Psychologists Press, Inc., Palo Alto, CA 94303 from *Introduction to Type* by Isabel Briggs Myers. Copyright 1993 by Consulting Psychologists Press. All rights reserved. Further reproduction is prohibited without the Publisher's written consent.)

1. Energising (direction of energy)

Extrovert (E)	Introvert (I)
• External	• Internal
• Outside thrust	• Inside pull
• Blurt it out	• Keep it in
• Breadth	• Depth
• People, things	• Ideas, thoughts
• Interaction	• Concentration
• Action	• Reflection
• Do-think-do	• Think-to-do

2. Attending (perception)

Sensing (S)	Intuition (N)
• The 5 senses	• 6th sense
• What is real	• What could be
• Practical	• Theoretical
• Present	• Future
• Facts	• Insights
• Using established skills	• Learning new skills
• Utility	• Novelty
• Step by step	• Leap around

3. Deciding (judgement)

Thinking (T)	Feeling (F)
• Head	• Heart
• Logical system	• Value system
• Objective	• Subjective
• Justice	• Mercy
• Critique	• Compliment
• Principles	• Harmony
• Reason	• Empathy
• Firm but fair	• Compassionate

4. Living (orientation to the outside world)

Judgement (J)	Perception (P)
• Planful	• Spontaneous
• Regulate	• Flow
• Control	• Adapt
• Settled	• Tentative
• Run one's life	• Let life happen
• Set goals	• Get data
• Decisive	• Open
• Organised	• Flexible

Exercise
- Think about yourself and someone with whom you have worked ineffectively – do you differ on any of these four dimensions? What might you have done to work better together? Consider arranging for you and your team to have your 'types' identified.

Briggs thought he was the best syndicate accounts manager, data analyst, economist, underwriter and plate spinner Finklestein Hooch & Krupp had ever employed.

Key point: Overcome your coaching blocks, or you'll never delegate

8. Finding and Avoiding your Coaching Blocks

In which Alex forgets all his coaching lessons

The champagne corks popped as the deal was finally signed. By acquiring Tubs-and-Cones International, Alex's company had completed the largest take-over in its history, and had become the biggest player in the world ice-cream market.

Alex was now in charge of the integration effort (Project Genesis) with a full-time team of 12 people. He felt confident that he could perform, with promotion virtually guaranteed. 'Senior manager after only 18 months with the company – not bad!' he mused.

He set to work, laying out a punishing schedule for himself and the team. There was much to be done: defining the new management structure, confirming likely cost savings and synergies, reassuring key customers, and double checking the financial implications of the acquisition.

* * *

Bob, still Alex's boss, was right to be concerned. He had noticed that Alex had virtually swaggered out of his office with the good news that he had landed the project management role. Alex was being just that bit too eager.

Because the other team members were not available immediately, Alex had used the intervening time to plan the team's activities in great detail. 'Hmm . . .' he thought, 'lots of data to be analysed on this project. I bet we'll also need to commission some market research, feed the information into a computer to identify the relevant market segments, then we can figure out which marketing channels to use for each type of product in each geographic region . . . .'

Unfortunately, Alex was not really a marketing expert; yet by the time the people from the Marketing Department arrived on the team, they found that Alex had mapped out exactly what they should be doing. Although Alex had made mistaken assumptions about the market, his style did not allow them to correct him. The people seconded from Finance and Operations had similar experiences.

So it was with a feeling of impending doom that the team left its first full meeting. Alex had not asked for any of their expert input, and had allocated all their tasks in extreme detail for the next two months. They were right to be worried. In the following weeks, Alex was in 'tell' mode most of the time. Moreover, with little team discussion, people found themselves duplicating each other's work, flying off at tangents, and generally becoming demotivated.

* * *

The phone on Alex's desk rang from somewhere beneath the piles of papers which had clearly cost the lives of several Amazonian rain forests. 'Hello, Alex, it's Bob here – could you drop by for a minute? Yes, now.' Bob looked up from his desk as Alex walked in. 'Alex, I've got some good news, and some bad news – which would you like first?'

Alex elected for the good news first, which was that the Acquisition Review Committee had been reasonably pleased with the progress of Alex's team so far. 'However,' continued Bob, 'we're all worried about whether the rest of the work on this project will get done. You used to be regarded as a good coach and manager, but you seem to have slipped into a mode of real "micro management" over the last month. Several of your team members have even asked to be moved off your team. If you're going to turn into a "people-eater" there's no way you will be able to manage *this* project. What's gone wrong?'

'There's just not enough time to coach people on this project,' shrugged Alex, who went on to explain all the problems which needed to be addressed. 'In addition,' he continued, 'with only three more months for this project to run, I really don't think that any time I invest in coaching now will generate a major benefit.'

Bob disagreed. 'You have hit a coaching block, Alex. You'll have to overcome it – and fast.' Bob went on to explain that managers sometimes run into situations where they feel reluctant to coach. The block most frequently encountered is where the manager says, 'There just isn't enough time to coach or to provide feedback'. However, this is normally an excuse for 'I need to be in complete control – I cannot risk delegating'. Clearly, there are times when this response may be appropriate. But too often these situations are exactly the ones in which the manager needs to do everything possible to unleash the full power of the people with whom s/he is working.

'Well, how do I get around this block . . . and what are the other types of coaching block?' asked Alex.

'You're good at planning – why not plan some *coaching*?' Bob replied, handing Alex a brief note (reproduced on the next two pages). 'I really want you to work on your people skills, Alex. You're strong in all other dimensions of management, but this could really hold you back,' he added.

* * *

Deep down, Alex knew he'd have to do some serious self-examination – other aspects of his life were not going well. For example, over the preceding few months, his relationship with his girlfriend Rachel had become very strained. She had accused him of never listening to her, and of always trying to organise everything. He had even insisted on telling her exactly what birthday present she should give her mother. The end had come last week when she had eventually left him, and had returned to an old flame. Perhaps he had become a 'control freak' after all.

Late that night he called Sarah for advice. She was on temporary assignment in Hong Kong, and the difference between time zones meant that she would now be at the office.

Working Around Coaching Blocks

Sometimes we do not take up opportunities to coach other people, even though we are well-intentioned. Why is this, and what can we do about it?

A major organisation recently conducted research in this area. It compared the coaching behaviour of 80 managers with their in-depth psychological profiles. This identified: (1) four typical 'rationales' that the managers sometimes used to 'allow' themselves not to coach; (2) the real underlying reasons for not coaching; and (3) how they could overcome these blocks (see the chart opposite).

For example, those managers who claimed they did not have enough time to coach were typically people with an unusually high need to control their environment and the people around them.

While the origins of this trait were buried somewhere in the managers' psychology, the exact cause was irrelevant. The important observation was that, for those managers, the best route into coaching was to 'control' how and when they would provide coaching and feedback.

There were three other frequently encountered coaching 'blocks', each with its own likely remedy, as shown on the opposite page.

Coaching Blocks and Ways Around Them

Typical 'rationale' for not coaching	Possible 'real' reason	Possible entry into coaching
1. 'Not enough time to coach'	I need to be in complete control	Agree very specifically when and how coaching will happen
2. 'Coachee won't respond, anyway'	I'm frightened I can't do it	Ask coachee how s/he would like to receive feedback/ coaching
3. 'The task won't suffer if I don't coach'	If I ignore it, the problem will go away	Reassess your ability to become a true leader
4. 'I might hurt them'	They won't like me	Start where it is safe – someone with whom you get on well, or someone who is good, but could be great

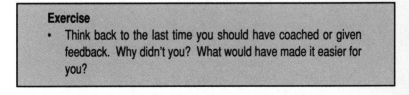

Exercise
- Think back to the last time you should have coached or given feedback. Why didn't you? What would have made it easier for you?

Ted's inability to distinguish giving advice from delivering criticism holds up the project at an important stage . . .

Key point: 'Instant payoff' coaching *can* work, but only if delivered well

9. Coaching in a Hurry

In which Alex is still out of control, and benefits from a dose of instant payoff coaching

Following his discussion with Bob, Alex had set himself the aspiration of overcoming his coaching block, and so unleashing the team's full potential. He was determined not to be a 'control freak' from now on!

Nevertheless, he did know more about the ice-cream industry than anyone else in the company. Very soon, the temptation was too strong. Six weeks later, Alex still found himself suffering from his inability to let go of any part of Project Genesis. Things came to a head halfway through the gruelling schedule which Alex had set for integrating the European manufacturing operations of the newly created ice-cream empire.

Most of the joint manufacturing operations were in France, and Alex had thought that Tom (who had continued to work with Alex on Project Genesis, after the original Project Quest) could carry out the interviews there. Alex would go along to the first few interviews, then Tom could carry on by himself, while Alex spent more time on the marketing strategy.

Unfortunately, Alex had early on come to the conclusion that Tom could not do the interviews by himself. Rather than cancel the planned meetings, Alex had handled them all himself, writing up the meeting notes late into the night, then spending an hour or two on the marketing strategy.

One particular night, he had a bad dream: he was doomed to be on a very long project which involved interviewing everyone in the phone book whose telephone number was a prime number. It took a whole year to do this, by which time a new phone book had been published . . .

Alex was working too hard, and he knew it. He went to see Bob, his boss. 'We've got a real problem on the European integration, Bob. We need to renegotiate the timetable.'

* * *

Bob knew that it would be impossible to change the timetable: everything had to be ready for the peak sales of ice cream next summer. He also did not want to volunteer more of his own time to the project, because of his other commitments. He had to help Alex build his confidence that there were other ways forward, but he was due to get in a cab to the airport in ten minutes.

'What's the problem?' he asked, remembering the instant payoff coaching technique that he had recently picked up from the new company-wide coaching programme.

'Well,' Alex began, 'Tom really isn't skilled at interviewing, and I'm nervous about the reaction to him of our new French subsidiary. I can't see how I can help him, as well as manage the overall project, as well as complete my own work on the marketing strategy . . . it's simply too much. Given the enormous value of this project to the company, surely we can get agreement to adding another team member – just for a month or two?'

Bob paused before responding. He thought that there may be a better solution – one which would encourage Alex to be less of a 'control freak'. 'Let's explore the issue more fully. Tell me what you would see if the problem was fixed; don't tell me how we could do it, just tell me what success would look like.'

Alex reflected for a moment. 'Well, Tom would have completed all the interviews, would have built relationships with the key executives in France, and would have drafted a report summarising his findings, which I could discuss with him a few days before the next steering group meeting . . .'

Alex looked visibly relieved but then panicked, 'But he isn't good enough, he . . .'

Bob stopped him. 'Before we examine Tom's abilities, tell me the obstacles between where we are now and where you said you'd like us to be.'

As Alex spoke, Bob simply listed the points on a flipchart. He didn't comment on the obstacles, but just asked Alex to look at the completed list, and to indicate where each obstacle lay – in himself, in someone else or in the situation.

Alex was surprised to see how many of the obstacles were in fact to do with himself, and that relatively few were to do with Tom's abilities. Bob didn't need to ask Alex what he was going to focus on as a next step; Alex volunteered. 'This is great. I can see a way through this without more people, if you would talk to the Chief Executive of the French subsidiary about his people's dismissive attitudes to Tom. We'll send Tom on a one-day interviewing course, and I'll see if I can come off the recruiting taskforce for just a couple of days.' As they ended their ten-minute session, Bob went off to the airport and Alex set off down the hall to find Tom.

*   *   *

Thereafter, Alex made great use of the instant payoff coaching technique which he had learnt from Bob.

Instant Payoff Coaching

Sometimes you do not have the time or knowledge to complete a full coaching discussion and really build someone's skills, but you do want to help someone who is 'stuck' to complete the task in question.

Using the model shown opposite, you can achieve this in as little as five minutes by helping your coachees to see that they too have some responsibility for the situation and that there *is* something they can do, however small.

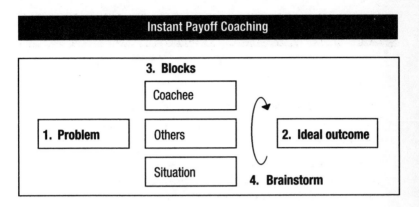

1. Ask the coachee to describe the current issue or problem, with specific examples and a small amount of relevant background.

2. Ask her/him to describe the outcome – paint as specific a 'picture' as possible of how things would be if s/he had sorted out the problem. Do not try to solve the problem, but note down any emerging ideas.

3. With the coachee, list all the obstacles/blocks that lie between 1 and 2. Sort them into three groups:

   • Blocks that exist in the coachee (lack of skill/knowledge, low motivation, attitude, etc.)

   • Blocks that exist in others (anxious customer, manager stressed and panicking, etc.)

   • Blocks in the situation (inadequate resources, shift in deadlines, etc.).

4. Jointly brainstorm ways around these blocks, and possible next steps. Agree an approach, actions and timing.

Exercise
• Try this on yourself. If it works, try it with the next person who asks for your advice.

Frankenstein makes a fundamental error in his 'Jump for Joy' programme.

Key point: Diagnose your coachee's will, not just skill

10. Taking Account of Others' Skill and Will

In which Alex learns about the Skill/Will matrix

'About time too,' thought Alex, as Bob gave him the official news of his promotion to senior manager.

'Of course,' added Bob, reading Alex's mind, 'you would have been promoted earlier – based on the project management skills you displayed by completing Project Genesis on time. But we had to be sure that you had the *people* skills needed at senior manager level. We had to be sure that you didn't stumble over your coaching block. After all, inventories can be managed, but people need to be led.'

Now, two years into his career with the company, Alex had five or six major initiatives to look after. He knew that in his new role he would have to be careful about how he allocated his time – there really was no way in which he could 'micro manage' all these initiatives at the same time. Fortunately, having seen the power of effective coaching, he had read up on the subject. This was the perfect opportunity to apply the Skill/Will matrix, and he reread the paragraphs from his coaching book.

In some ways, the idea of the Skill/Will matrix is simple, but it needs practice to apply it effectively. The overall concept is that you tailor your style of coaching and management to the skill and will of the person you are managing, bearing in mind the task they are trying to accomplish.

For example, if someone really is able to accomplish a given task, and they are motivated to complete it (i.e., high skill and high will), then the appropriate management style would be to Delegate.

> *However, if the person had low skill and low will – for the task in question – then you would need to be more Directive, at least initially. For high skill, low will – or vice versa – the manager should use Excite or Guide styles respectively.**

> *While this sounds simple in theory, there are two main challenges. First, you have to really diagnose the coachee's skill and will, without leaping to conclusions based on prejudice or accepting the coachee's frequent pretence to be 'high skill and high will' at everything. And second, you need to modify dynamically your management or coaching style, as the coachee builds both skill and will.*

Alex thought about Tom, who had now been with the company for about a year. Tom was in charge of the project to identify the company's next acquisition in the frozen food market. Alex knew that Tom was high on will: he was very keen on this role, having dropped enough hints to Alex that he wanted the assignment.

But Alex wasn't so sure about Tom's skill. Tom certainly had the creativity and flexibility which the new project might require. But Alex thought Tom was less strong in strategy and valuation analysis.

Rather than leaping to conclusions, however, Alex decided to have a frank discussion with Tom. He was careful to use genuinely open – as opposed to leading – questions, and to avoid an accusing tone of voice. This discussion confirmed Alex's initial thoughts, although he was relieved to discover that Tom had carried out several company valuations while with his previous employer.

'High will, fairly high skill' thought Alex. 'I can afford to Delegate and be fairly hands-off; but I had better make sure I provide a bit of Guidance in the area of strategy.'

* * *

Alex went through a similar process with the four other people who reported directly to him . . . one more Guide, two Delegates and a Direct. He felt relieved that he had things in perspective, and that he could now prioritise his time for the next month or so. Thereafter

---

* See Appendix 4 (page 110) for descriptions of these styles

he'd review progress to see whether he could use more of the Delegate style, to free up more time for himself!

Selecting an Appropriate Coaching Style
The Skill/Will Matrix

All too often, we assign a task to someone and the job does not quite get done well enough. Why is this?

One of the most likely reasons is that we have delegated the task to someone who is unwilling – or unable – to complete the job, and have then remained relatively 'hands-off' or uninvolved. Alternatively, we may have been 'hands-on' or directive with a capable person who was quite able to complete the assignment with little assistance from us; we just ended up demotivating her/him.

Consequently, whether you are 'coaching' or just 'managing', it is critical to match your style of interaction with the coachee's readiness for the task.

To help you do this, use the Skill/Will matrix:

- First, diagnose the coachee's skill and will to accomplish the task, as indicated on the opposite page

- Then use the matrix to identify the appropriate style of interaction – e.g., you would want to use 'Delegate' if your coachee was high in both skill and will

- Finally, agree with your coachee which style you will be using and for what reasons

A few observations:

- Ensure you are addressing the coachee's skill and will to execute the **specific** task in question – e.g., 'making presentations to the Board of Directors' rather than 'public speaking'

- If you are working with someone over a longer period, you will want them to increase in both will and skill. If they are successful in doing this, you will need gradually to adopt the appropriate styles en route to 'Delegate'

(The Skill/Will matrix is an adaptation by Keilty, Goldsmith & Co, Inc., of original work by Hersey and Blanchard.)

1. Diagnose whether the coachee's skill and will are high or low, for the specific task to be accomplished:
   - **Skill** depends on experience, training, understanding, role perception
   - **Will** depends on desire to achieve, incentives, security, confidence

2. Identify the appropriate coaching/management style – e.g., use 'Guide' if the coachee has high will but low skill for the task:

Skill/Will Matrix

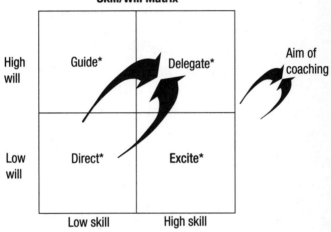

* See Appendix 4 (page 110) for details of each approach

3. Agree your intended approach with your coachee.

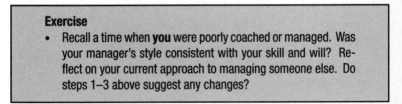

Exercise
- Recall a time when **you** were poorly coached or managed. Was your manager's style consistent with your skill and will? Reflect on your current approach to managing someone else. Do steps 1–3 above suggest any changes?

Doc Gilby, the Dentist, gained trust and built confidence through his use of Fluffywuffy the hand puppet . . . of course if that didn't work there was always Mr Slap Hammer . . .

Key point: Build genuine trust with the 'reluctant' coachee

11. Overcoming a Reluctance to Being Coached

In which Alex learns to overcome the reluctance of one of his coachees

Alex was muttering to himself as he walked down the corridor. Just when he had really begun to master some of the more advanced aspects of coaching, such as the Skill/Will matrix, he had had to endure yet another frustrating and unproductive discussion with Angus, the analyst who was working for Tom on the latest acquisition.

* * *

Despite the overwhelming temptation to blame Angus, Alex decided to be more constructive. Applying some self-coaching, he tried the GROW model (refer back to Chapter 6) on himself. 'What is my **Goal** here . . . to decide on one thing which might unlock my communication with Angus, so that I can deliver some vital feedback. What about the current **Reality**, then . . .' Alex began to recall his encounter with Angus.

'Angus, how are you doing?' Alex had asked as he had entered Angus's office.

'Fine,' had come the rather clipped response.

'Is there anything you would like my help on, while Tom is away on vacation?' In response to the shaken head, Alex had persevered, 'Are you absolutely sure that everything is under control – everything which you had agreed with Tom?'

'Absolutely.'

Tom had warned Alex that Angus tended to overestimate his ability, and that he was reluctant to ask for help. Tom had attributed this to the culture of Angus's previous company, where survival had depended on a continuous show of strength.

Alex offered Angus a chance. 'You *are* allowed to ask for help around here, you know.' Angus thanked him for the offer, promised to ask for help if needed, and pressed on with his work. As he reflected on the encounter, Alex was puzzled. Surely people knew that they could be open with him.

He thought back to the times when he had been in Angus's situation. As a more junior person, even Alex had been reluctant to disclose his own needs in new relationships with bosses and peers. He had felt that his 'admissions' might just be used against him. Alex realised that – in discussions with Angus – he had been relying purely on his *reputation* as a good coach. Perhaps Angus did not trust him.

'So,' thought Alex, 'if trust is the key, what are my **Options?** Let's see: (1) tell him it's OK, (2) ask someone else to tell him that I can be trusted, (3) let Tom worry about it . . .' None of the ideas seemed a likely winner. 'All right,' he mused, 'how do *I* assess whether I can trust someone?'

As he was jotting down his thoughts he suddenly remembered a simple idea that he had once read about. This was that you could look at a relationship in terms of an 'emotional bank account', or how much credit (or debit) of goodwill existed between the two people. With strangers, for example, you might have no store of goodwill, and so it would naturally be difficult to get them to do something for you, since there was no reserve of goodwill upon which to draw.

Alex realised that his 'emotional bank account' with Angus was probably overdrawn. Alex had recently made some last-minute requests of the team, which had made for some long hours. He also recalled that Angus's father – who lived three hours' drive away – was extremely unwell, and that the weekend working made visits difficult. He also realised that he didn't know very much about Angus's aspirations for himself. It now seemed obvious to Alex that the problem lay not so much in his lacking skills as a coach, but rather in his lacking any real relationship with Angus. Having reviewed his options, Alex **Wrapped up**; he knew what to do next.

He found out more about Angus from reading through his last annual appraisal. He made sure that Angus could get home on the following weekend. And he persuaded Angus to go out for a quick drink with him, during which Alex talked about his own career with the company, how he had found it hard to trust new bosses at first, and how difficult it had been to overcome his doubts. He listened carefully to Angus's description of his previous company, and to his fears and aspirations for the job he was now in.

When Alex felt that the moment was right, he asked Angus how he would like to receive feedback or guidance in the future, should the opportunity arise. He stressed that he meant informal, on-the-job feedback, not the kind that ends up in personnel files. With a more open, trusting relationship, it was easy for Angus to ask for the support he wanted, and he was even willing to *ask* for Alex and Tom to monitor more closely tasks which were new to him, or of particularly high risk.

* * *

Alex reflected that perhaps the foundation of all successful coaching is an open, trusting relationship with a healthy reservoir of goodwill on both sides.

Dealing with a Reluctance to be Coached

You may feel that someone would benefit from your coaching, but that s/he appears reluctant to accept your help.

To make progress, you will need to diagnose why the potential coachee is resisting you. He or she may be reluctant to accept any form of coaching by *anyone*, or may just be reluctant to have *you* as a coach at the current time.

To take appropriate initiatives, you will need to delve to at least one further level of diagnosis (see opposite page).

Dealing with Reluctance	
Coachee's mindset	**Options for the coach**
Intrinsic reluctance to be coached	
• Unwillingness to admit scope for improvement (in general or in the specific coaching topic)	• Diagnose the coachee's barriers • Emphasise factual evidence for the need to improve ('push' strategy) or . . . • Break through by asking the coachee to coach you ('pull' strategy)
• Mistrust of the organisation	• Build the trust
• Temporary lack of available time	• Agree a later session
Reluctance to be coached by you	
• Unhelpful historical relationship with you	• Attempt to 'bury the hatchet'*
• Major difference between her/ his style and yours	• Discuss explicitly, and accept, the 'style' differences if possible* (see Chapter 7)
• Perceived nature of your role in the organisation as being 'highly evaluative'	• Be explicit about your role – e.g., whether you determine the coachee's remuneration
	• Stress that the coaching is 'non-evaluative'*

* Or suggest an alternative coach if all else fails

Exercise
• Identify your most 'reluctant' coachee. Develop a plan using the above pointers.

Key point: You can't motivate others if they can't see you

12. Motivating

In which Alex finds that he can be a good motivator after all

A few weeks later, Alex reflected on his two-and-a-half years with the company. He was glad he had joined the firm: he seemed to be well-regarded, had been promoted with reasonable speed, and he admired the people-oriented culture which, he felt sure, had something to do with the company's performance, which exceeded the industry's average.

In his senior manager role he had thought a bit about the topic of motivating others. There didn't seem to be many books on the subject, so he had gradually pieced together tips from watching what other particularly good managers did.

As he thought about Mary – who had joined his division 18 months ago, and for whom he was preparing an end-of-year appraisal session – he wondered how he could apply the three lessons he had learnt about motivation. These were: (1) help the coachee to understand consciously her/his current level of motivation; (2) help the coachee to fashion a really convincing vision of how well s/he could perform; and (3) support the coachee in her/his efforts through praise and coaching.

* * *

Alex had spent the first 15 minutes of his meeting with Mary reviewing her performance so far. It had not been easy, since she had been 'low skill, low will' on many of her recent assignments. Alex now decided to switch direction for the last 15 minutes of the meeting.

'Mary, it seems to me that you are caught in a negative cycle. You start off lacking confidence in your abilities; this leads you to make hesitant attempts at the tasks on which you are engaged; as a result, you deliver below your real potential; and then you receive less praise than you would hope for. This in turn just exacerbates your lack of confidence.' Alex sketched out the cycle.*

'You know, Alex,' she responded, 'I think you're right. I'd never thought about it this way before; everything just seemed all tangled up. But how can I break out of this cycle into a more positive one?'

'Let's think about something at which you could be really good . . . any suggestions?'

They discussed a few options, and discarded some which didn't seem relevant enough to Mary's mainstream work activities. In the end, they decided that Mary was going to become the best person in the entire company at making presentations. Alex thought the objective was stretching, but achievable. Although Mary was a bit shy, she was a key figure in the local amateur dramatic group.

'Now, how are we going to get there?' asked Alex. Mary had perked up as the result of the preceding discussion, but now gulped and paled. Alex bit his lip and resisted the temptation to dive in and rescue her. Eventually, Mary came up with a surprisingly rich stream of her own ideas, ranging from making the prize draw at the departmental Christmas party, through to running the induction session for people who were just joining the company.

'And what type of help do you think you need?' probed Alex.

'I think I can handle most of this myself!' responded a re-energised Mary, whose ideas ranged from taking a one-day course in presenting herself with more impact, through to noting the presentation techniques of famous people as they appeared on television. 'All I'd ask is that you give me some feedback whenever you see me make a presentation.'

* * *

---

* See page 67

'What on earth have you done to Mary while I've been away?' It was the long-lost Sarah standing at Alex's door.

Sarah had just returned from her posting to the company's Hong Kong operation. She had worked with Mary before. But now, several weeks after the annual appraisal session with Alex, Mary seemed a different person.

It turned out that Mary was making real progress in building her presentation skills. But – perhaps more importantly – her growing self-confidence in this area was already spilling over into other areas of her work. She was indeed becoming a much more motivated person. Alex was beginning to think that the time he had invested during the appraisal session had been well worthwhile, and he was glad that he had not confined himself to merely running through the company's standard appraisal form with Mary.

'Well, how were things in Hong Kong?' enquired Alex. 'I tried to call you several times, but you had always just left for some part of South East Asia.'

'It's a long story,' said Sarah. 'But I really learned a lot about managing in an environment with a different culture.'

Motivation

The golden rules of motivation:

1. **Know where your coachees are** in the cycle of motivation or demotivation shown opposite.

2a. **Work on their confidence,** if they are in the uppermost cycle, as it's about the only thing you can affect directly. Do this by:

   - Working with them to develop a vision of how good they could be at completing a specific task, or playing a specific role

   - Recognising that improved performance in an area which might not be critical to their mainstream activities usually has very positive spinoff benefits to their 'core' activities.

2b. **Work on praise** if they are in the lower cycle.

3. **Identify their needs for support and/or training,** even if it is to be provided by the coachee themself or by a third party.

4. **Know what most motivates your coachees.** Everyone has different motivating factors (see Appendix 5, page 112).

Negative Cycle of Demotivation

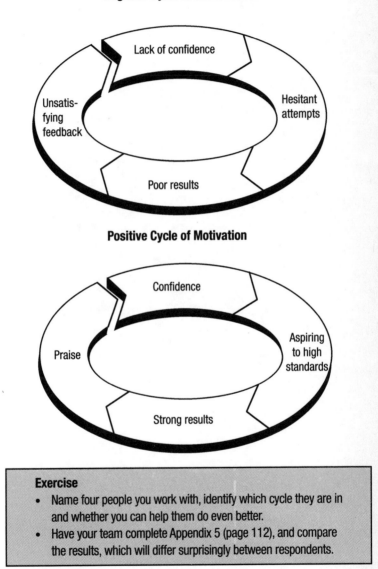

Positive Cycle of Motivation

Exercise
- Name four people you work with, identify which cycle they are in and whether you can help them do even better.
- Have your team complete Appendix 5 (page 112), and compare the results, which will differ surprisingly between respondents.

Although Friday afternoon 'Postboy Racing' had been a popular pastime where Lars came from, he still had quite a bit to learn about Frimly and Booth office culture . . .

Key point: Take time to anticipate cultural differences

13. Recognising Cultural Differences

In which Alex discovers how cultural differences affect coaching

Alex found himself pinned to his seat as flight MA245 took off, ultimate destination Moravia, via Paris. Project Genesis – the integration of Cones-and-Tubs into the company – was nearing completion, but the company had just completed a further acquisition to make it the largest ice-cream producer in Eastern Europe.

The following morning he found himself in the boardroom of the new Moravian subsidiary, ready for his first full meeting with the local management team. Alex knew the meeting was critical, and knew that it would not be easy to manage this far-flung arm of the company from London. So he had to take every opportunity to build the credibility of 'Head Office' as soon as possible.

Consequently, he had decided to have dinner with the local Strategy Director, Jan, the previous evening to agree how they would run the management meeting. Jan would start off with the agreed presentation on the benefits of the 'merger', then there would be a free-format discussion, followed by a tour of the plant. Alex had met with Jan only once before, but had gained the impression that he was very pushy. So Alex had spent a few minutes gently coaching him on how to 'soften' his style.

* * *

Alex cringed as Jan delivered his presentation to the assembled managers. 'Oh no,' thought Alex, 'what a disaster!'

He knew that Moravians typically pulled no punches. They communicated in a very forthright manner. But surely Jan was going too far. What about the coaching session which Alex had had with him the night before?

Why was Jan not using the softer approach which they had discussed? And what had happened to the comments on which they had agreed as face-saving measures for the local Chief Executive?

Alex searched in vain for a way to intercede as Jan increased the tempo. He felt the perspiration on his brow. 'At least,' he thought, 'I know how frank to be in my feedback to Jan as soon as this meeting is over!'

Perhaps it was the pressure, perhaps it was the local Moravian brew he had consumed the night before, perhaps it was the jet lag, but Alex seemed to lose touch with reality for what seemed like only an instant.

The next thing he knew, the audience was on its feet – a standing ovation!

* * *

Later that day, Alex reflected on how he might have managed things differently. Although things had worked out OK in the end, Alex concluded that he'd be more careful next time he coached someone from an obviously different culture. He would think in advance about the most important cultural differences between himself, the coachee, and the coaching context.

For example, Alex thought he should have listened more to Jan over dinner, perhaps discussing openly the cultural issues relating to the forthcoming meeting – rather than presumptuously coaching him on how to *soften* his style. Nevertheless, if Alex did have to coach Jan again, he would probably be much more frank in his advice, to match Jan's cultural background.

Furthermore, Jan – like Alex – was used to operating in an environment without much hierarchy. However, if Jan had typically been more deferential to his 'bosses', Alex reflected that he would have had to exercise care that a brainstormed idea was not interpreted as a direct order.

Similarly, the meaning – and importance – of 'teamwork' can differ significantly or subtly between cultures, with implications for the senior manager who is attempting to build a team.

Alex boarded the Boeing 727 that would take him home. He was glad that he'd decided to stop over in Paris for the weekend, and was even more delighted to have discovered that Sarah would be there too. He wanted to discuss her experiences in Hong Kong, and compare notes on how to be an effective manager in an unfamiliar culture.

Cultural Differences

When coaching someone from a different culture, s/he may well act – or react – differently from what you are used to:

- Cultural differences do not arise only from national, racial or religious origins – e.g., people new to your organisation may still be heavily influenced by the culture of their previous employer

- These differences can result in higher or lower levels of perceived performance, and in more or less need for – and acceptance of – feedback

- When working with multinational teams, or individuals from cultures different from yours, be **explicit** with yourself, and ideally with them, about the implications of cultural differences

- Above all, commit to building shared expectations – in terms of management style, adherence to deadlines, frequency of progress checks, need for creativity, etc.

For further details, see *Cultures and Organisations* by Geert Hofstede.

Four Cultural Dimensions

Cultures – both national and organisational – differ along many dimensions. Four of the most important ones are indicated below:

Dimension	Implication for the coach
• **Directness** (get to the point *versus* imply the messages)	Tailor style of feedback appropriately
• **Hierarchy** (follow orders *versus* engage in debate)	Position coaching relationship carefully *vis à vis* organisational reporting relationship
• **Consensus** (dissent is accepted *versus* unanimity is needed)	Select from full repertoire of ask/tell styles – see pages 8 and 9
• **Individualism** (individual winners *versus* team effectiveness)	Reflect on focus of coaching – e.g., whether or not to focus on teamwork

Exercise
• Recall the last time you had difficulty working with someone from another culture. What went wrong? Why? Could you have avoided the problem? Would it have been worth doing?

As Dr Peterson and Professor Forbes slug it out over who has first use of the Nobo board, the rest of the UN Peace Mission start laying odds . .

Key point: Set up teams well

14. Starting Teams Well

In which Alex discovers that he has become a recognised team leader

By the time Alex turned up at the party to celebrate Sarah's promotion, the room was already full. Sarah was both highly popular and widely respected as a manager, so attendance was high.

Glass in hand, Alex squeezed away from the crowded bar, and found space within listening distance of a small group of people. One of them, Tom, had recently joined Alex's taskforce which was developing the company's three-year plan, and the others seemed to be quizzing him. Alex eavesdropped attentively from his position behind the pot plant.

* * *

'What's it like working with this Alex guy?' asked someone. 'I hear he sets a pretty punishing schedule, and I know he used to be a real people-eater.'

'I think that's a thing of the past,' replied Tom. 'We just had a kickoff meeting on this planning taskforce of his, and I must say that Alex really seems to be a good people manager, as well as being smart.'

'How do you mean?'

'Well, he had set the meeting up really well. There are five of us on this taskforce, and he'd sent us all a copy of the work plan which he'd drafted, several days in advance.'

'What's the big deal about that?' asked another member of the group.

'The point is, he made it very clear that he'd welcome our comments on the plan,' Tom continued. 'He must have done a bit of research on each of us, too – even the people seconded in from other departments – because he sort of knew which areas each of us could best comment on.

'Anyway, we got together for the meeting, and he gave a really convincing speech about the importance of the work – he managed to build a genuine spirit of camaraderie.

'And then he handed out copies of the last annual appraisal which *his* boss had given *him* – not just the good bits, but the things at which he's meant to be improving.'

'But why on earth did he do that?' asked someone else.

'Well, he didn't tell us why in so many words, but the effect was quite powerful, because it made people really open up when he asked each of *us* to explain what we wanted personally to get out of this project. And we really believed him when he said that this was going to be a team in which we gave each other a lot of feedback, and helped each other out if we needed to.

'We even spent five minutes on which parts of the project looked the most busy, to check that the inevitable late hours weren't going to interfere too much with our personal lives.

'Then we talked through our roles and responsibilities. You know, he actually listened to what we had to say, and we rearranged that draft work plan quite a bit. When we left the meeting, we all knew pretty much what we were meant to do, and felt that this was going to be a real team effort. We even agreed to have a team appraisal session* in three weeks' time, to check that our teamwork was up to scratch.'

'You don't need a PhD in rocket science to do that kind of thing,' quipped a more cynical bystander.

'No, you don't,' replied Tom, 'but tell me if you've ever had a team meeting like that. And that thing about sharing his own annual

---

* See Appendix 6 (page 114)

appraisal – the only reason it had impact was that it took some courage on his part.'

* * *

Alex could not suppress a self-contented smirk as he sidled away to find Sarah. 'So that was what "corridor talk" sounded like first hand . . !' he thought. 'And it's true, you don't necessarily need to be a rocket scientist to be a great team leader.'

He also thought about how valuable his skills in *one-to-one* coaching had been when it came to building and managing a team.

Coaching in the Team Context

Some teams work hard, have fun and get the job done. Other teams are miserable and ineffective, despite the fact that all the team members are working twice as hard as normal. Why is this?

In their book *The Wisdom of Teams*, Jon Katzenbach and Douglas Smith identified the six basic requirements for good teamwork illustrated below. While it is beyond our scope to address each of these basics, let's review the one most related to coaching – the well-defined working approach.

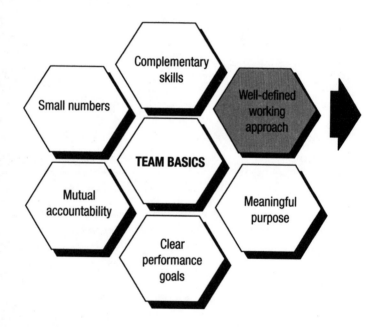

Define Your Approach

A well-defined working approach is integral to effective teamwork and essential for a positive coaching environment.

Constructive characteristics include:

1. The leader holds a half-day meeting within the first two weeks, to agree ground rules and 'team charter' – e.g.,
   - Individuals' objectives
   - Working hours and likely 'crunch' periods

2. Individuals discuss personal needs for skills development openly and early
   - Set example by sharing last personal performance review with team
   - Set clear expectations for feedback

3. The whole team participates in drafting workplan

4. All team members feel comfortable providing and receiving ongoing feedback and 'blowing the whistle' if necessary

5. The team reviews how it is working every six weeks, or more frequently if needed, or after major milestones (e.g., after publishing a report).

Exercise
- Consider points 1–5 in the context of your current project and suggest/take corrective action if needed.

Armed to the teeth with his sixth sense and no torch, Ted presses on.

Key point: Coaches work with observable facts, not just 'gut feel'

15. Coaching Caveats

In which Alex goes too far with pop psychology

Alex had just been on a long vacation, to celebrate his fourth anniversary with the company. He had returned with a tan and a general feeling of well-being – particularly since his relationship with his new girlfriend had endured its first holiday test.

He ploughed through his in-tray with the help of his secretary, and as she was leaving he asked her for an update on the rumour, scandal and gossip from the office grapevine.

'Not much to report,' she began, 'It's been pretty quiet. All I've really heard is that Tim and Mary have had a bit of a bust-up.'

Mary was one of Alex's most able managers. She was spending a lot of time with Tim, from the marketing department, on a taskforce to revamp the company's research and development process. Although progress had been excellent, Alex had noticed that there had been some friction between the two of them.

'Time for a coaching session,' thought Alex, recalling the GROW framework which he had used so successfully over the years.

He met with Mary and they agreed that teamwork would be a good topic to discuss.

'How are you getting on with Tim?' asked Alex.

'Not too well,' responded Mary, 'we just don't seem to be on the same wavelength.'

Mary thought for a moment. 'Actually, we get on OK when there are just two of us. The friction seems to arise when there are other people in the room.'

Alex was sure he knew what was happening. He'd noticed that Mary had been very competitive in the company's recent annual softball tournament. Mary's problems with Tim conveniently confirmed Alex's hypothesis that she felt a need to assert herself when the audience grew larger than one.

'Do you sometimes feel a need to prove yourself in meetings with Tim, particularly when there are other people present?' Alex knew he was taking a chance, but he had a strong hunch that he was on the right track.

Mary looked suspiciously at Alex. 'Well, er . . . no, not really.'

'And did you feel competitive towards your brother when you were younger?' Alex continued.

Now Mary was *really* beginning to wonder what was happening. She glanced nervously around the room, noticing as she did so several well-thumbed books by Freud lying on the bookshelf. 'Actually,' Mary replied politely, 'I've always got on very well with my family.'

Alex pursued the point for a few more minutes until a call from abroad interrupted their meeting. It was Mary's chance to escape from the amateur psychologist's couch, and she took it.

* * *

Within a few days, Mary had resolved her problem with Tim. When Alex noticed the change he had a chat with Mary, and was surprised to find that their problems had arisen purely from a few specific misunderstandings. Then he thought back to his ineffective coaching session, and realised that he might have missed the point.

Perhaps it was inappropriate to delve too deeply into psychology. 'A little learning is a dangerous thing . . .' he mused. Next time he would listen more, and focus on the facts of the situation, taking them more at face value.

However, Alex had another problem which he was to discover the next day, and which would take several months of hard effort to sort out. In the period prior to his vacation he had spent so much time on coaching, motivating and feeding back to people that he had taken his eye off the underlying business issues. Some tough decisions had been called for. But, rather than take those decisions himself, he had delegated them to his teams. 'After all,' he had thought, 'my teams are *empowered*.' But unfortunately he had over-delegated the process of resolving several important strategic issues.

Coaching Caveats

When helping to build skills, great coaches – in contrast to great psychologists – typically do not delve deeply into the coachee's pysche. They work with, and provide feedback on, **perceived** behaviours and actions.

By way of analogy, we know how to switch channels on a TV set without knowing the details of the circuits inside. Consequently, bear in mind the overall guidelines for coaching indicated on the opposite page.

Furthermore, the skilled business manager – unlike the 'empowerment gone mad' coach – knows where to inject a dose of firm decision-making.

1. Don't become too 'psychological'.

Do	Don't
• Focus on helping the coachee with specific tasks	• Search for psychological problems which 'might' exist
• Be business-like and frank	• Try to be 'nice'
• Check you are addressing a real issue	• Miss the point
• Moderate the amount and depth of your coaching	• Overcoach
• Refer people with major personal problems to a qualified counsellor	• Bite off more than you can chew

2. Don't lose sight of strategic and operational issues which need your decisive action.

'I'm glad we had this little chat, Eddie, it turns out you're not the sneaky, snivelling, crying-in-the-toilets type I'd mistaken you for – when you get back to your office order yourself a new swivel chair, like mine . . .'

Key point: Providing 'upward' feedback to the boss can have its benefits

16. Giving Feedback Upwards

In which Alex discovers that it's easy to provide upward feedback, and that it can be rewarding

Alex had eventually resolved those strategic issues which he had let slip several months ago. But, with only six weeks to go until the shareholders' Annual General Meeting, he was growing nervous.

He was supposed to be helping Peter, the Chairman, with his speech, but whenever they met they always seemed to end up wasting a lot of time. First, Peter was rather disorganised and took ages to retrieve relevant papers from accidental hiding places. Second, people who happened to be passing Peter's office tended to just drop by and interrupt their meetings.

'Boy,' thought Alex as the fourth person in as many minutes knocked on the door, 'Peter could really use some feedback and coaching on time management and personal organisation. I wonder if anyone has ever mentioned anything to him in the past.'

As their meeting eventually drew to a close, Alex moved towards the door, plucked up courage, and turned to Peter. 'By the way, the company-wide coaching programme which we launched several years ago seems to be going really well. In fact, I've found the upward feedback which I've received has been very helpful – not just soft stuff, but suggestions that have really increased my effectiveness. How have you found it?'

'I must admit I haven't really had time to ask for any feedback, although I know the programme is meant to be for everyone.'

Alex paused in case Peter felt like inviting him to share his observations, but he waited in vain. He took a slightly deeper breath than normal and feigned nonchalance. 'Of course, we *could* just take a few minutes at the end of our next meeting if you'd like any suggestions from me,' he volunteered. The Chairman was apparently receptive, and Alex made a mental note to gather his thoughts prior to next week's rendezvous.

* * *

As that next meeting ended, Alex girded his loins. 'Well,' he began, 'how about that upward feedback?'

'I'm not sure I've got time for a discussion now,' replied Peter.

'But perhaps there are ways for you to actually create more time for yourself,' continued Alex undaunted. 'I've been giving it some thought.' The Chairman looked up, surprised but intrigued.

Alex said that he had a few ideas which might be helpful, but decided (remembering to use his full repertoire of ask/tell styles) to ask Peter what he thought would be the most useful area to cover. Peter was definitely interested in the topic of time management.

Alex suggested that they focus on the 45-minute meeting which they had just concluded, to see whether there were any clues to greater effectiveness.

After some discussion, Peter volunteered that he really should have his secretary set up a better filing system; that way he wouldn't spend ages looking for lost papers. They also brainstormed a further 20 ideas, all of which had some merit.

Just when Peter thought they had finished the discussion, Alex decided to broach what he was afraid would be the most sensitive area. He knew that Peter liked to maintain a strict 'open-door policy', but Alex was sure that the frequent interruptions which had frustrated him during the last three-quarters of an hour probably continued all day.

'Just a final thought, Peter; how about asking your secretary to screen out more of the people who drop by on a casual basis? I'm sure that would save you a lot of time, by allowing you to concentrate on one thing at a time. For example, we must have had 15 interruptions in the last 45 minutes. I know you like to have an open-door policy, but there is a difference between the door being ajar and it being agape!'

'Well, Alex, I always like people to feel they can contact me whenever they need to.'

'Yes,' responded Alex, 'but the result is that everyone who has ever met with you (and therefore been interrupted by others) feels entirely at home "getting their own back" and making up for the time they lost in their original meeting with you, through interrupting the next person you are seeing.' Alex realised he was going all out, and wondered how Peter would respond.

Peter was genuinely surprised – he had no idea of the dynamic which his open-door policy had set up. However, he balked at the prospect of forgoing his previously enshrined principle.

Having gone this far, Alex was not about to give up. 'Why don't you try an experiment for one week, Peter. After all, what's the worst that could happen?'

* * *

Peter did try it for a week. It worked, and he suddenly found himself with much more time than he'd ever had.

He went to find Alex. 'I just wanted to thank you for the "upward" feedback. That open-door policy worked when I started the company 30 years ago, but now we're a large multinational company. You were right to point out that the door should be "ajar not agape". Actually, you've prompted me to revamp a number of my other working habits, too.'

'Good chap, that Alex,' muttered the Chairman to himself as he headed off down the corridor.

Establishing an Effective Environment for Upward Feedback

Giving upward feedback is the same as giving feedback downwards, or 'sideways' to peers, provided you establish an explicit contract with your 'boss' to do so.

- Most people really appreciate constructive, timely, actionable and sensitively delivered feedback. However, you may sometimes feel that it is more difficult to deliver than it really is.

- Creating an environment and relationship which supports mutual giving and receiving of feedback is best done at the beginning of a task or working relationship, before there is any actual feedback to be given.

Useful ways to position the offer

- Would you like to receive feedback? If so, about what in particular, and in what form?

- If I have any observations about you which I think might be helpful to you or your team, how would you like me to communicate them?

- Is there any part of a specific task on which we are collaborating where feedback from me would be particularly helpful?

- It feels nerve-wracking to give feedback to you because you are so busy/tired/preoccupied/focused. How can I best get through to you in these situations?

Exercise
- At the beginning of your next piece of work, agree with your 'boss' how you will handle upward feedback.

17. Mentoring

In which Alex discovers that he is a mentor

With the Annual General Meeting out of the way, Alex had – in addition to his many other roles within the company – resumed his involvement in recruiting. He and several colleagues were discussing a candidate; it was time for the vote. All those who believed that the company should offer Donald the job were to raise their hands. Alex's hand went up, along with everyone else's.

He felt that Donald would be a great addition to the company. Alex thought that he had a few rough edges, but that these could be smoothed off fairly easily. Like Alex four years earlier, Donald's first position would be as manager of strategic planning.

* * *

A month later, Alex found himself as the official mentor to Donald, in the new company-wide mentoring programme. As no-one really knew what a mentor was meant to do, beyond taking the 'mentee' out for a quick welcoming lunch, Alex decided to go back to first principles in his search for an answer.

He thumbed through his dictionary:

Mentor. *A guide, a wise friend and counsellor. In Homer's* Odyssey, *Mentor was an old friend of Odysseus to whom the latter entrusted his home and his son Telemachus. The goddess Minerva assumed the form of Mentor to help Telemachus in his search for Odysseus who had left Ithaca for Troy.*

'Well what on earth does one do to become a guide, a wise and faithful counsellor,' he thought, 'short of becoming a classical deity?'

Over the next few months, Alex discovered that being a mentor was a lot like being a coach. First, there were times when the mentor could help the mentee to raise her/his spirits – and aspirations. Sometimes this involved using the skills of motivation that Alex had picked up earlier in his career; at other times Alex merely had a discussion that helped Donald to stand back from the problems of the moment, and to see his work and life in a broader context.

Then there were the times when Alex just provided a listening ear. He knew that Donald did not necessarily want Alex to help him with a specific problem, nor to log a concern 'officially'. Donald merely wanted to get something off his chest, and to know that someone senior cared enough to listen.

Sometimes Alex did need to shift into a more hands-on role, helping Donald to think through his options. These discussions normally focused on broader career issues, rather than the more task-specific issues addressed by a coach.

On other occasions, Alex provided information which Donald might not easily have gained from other sources – such as when he explained the company's emerging strategy in East Asia, and how Donald might use his knowledge of Mandarin to further his career.

Finally, there were times when Alex was the only person who would take on the task of advising Donald on a few changes in style which 'might not go amiss'. Like the time when Donald had started to wear green suits with pink shirts and brown shoes: it wasn't against company policy, but it didn't exactly enhance his credibility. And no-one else had felt like giving the feedback.

Alex had also learned to *avoid* playing certain roles which, at first glance, might appear to be part of a mentor's job description. For example, he had become very careful not to wade in with lots of advice. There were times when he was too far removed from the specific facts of a complicated situation to know what the correct answer was. It was then that he focused on helping Donald to come up with his own answers – just as the effective parent helps the child to become a problem-solver rather than a follower of 'advice-interpreted-as-orders'.

Alex also tried to avoid being a 'rescuer'. He knew that it would not help Donald in the long run if he 'took over' any of Donald's problems. For example, Donald was having a problem with his boss, who was a close friend of Alex's. It would have been easy for Alex to have a quiet word with his friend, but he resisted the temptation. He knew that Donald would learn more from figuring out and implementing the answer for himself. Donald would also have more confidence to solve a similar problem next time without having to turn to Alex.

* * *

Later, Alex reflected on the time he had spent mentoring Donald. He hadn't spent too many hours on it, but there were certainly other things for which he could have used the time. He concluded that there *were* some intangible benefits to being a mentor, such as those which Sarah had described in her article in the company magazine several years ago, but that was about it.

Just as Alex was turning his attention to other matters, Donald turned up. 'Alex, I've never really thanked you for all your advice. I just want you to know that you have had a real impact on me. You have even helped me indirectly with my relationship with my girlfriend. I'm not sure if you know, but she's the Chairman's daughter, and we're going to get married. I've already told my future father-in-law what a great guy you are.'

'Well,' thought Alex, 'perhaps there is such a thing as divine justice, after all.'

* * *

Alex cleared his desk, remembering to take with him his hand-held dictating machine, in case he had any unusual ideas while on vacation. He had completed all his preparations for the meeting of the Board which would take place in his absence.

On his way home he picked up the airline tickets that would take him to Greece . . .

Mentoring and coaching are very similar activities. The only real difference is that the coach focuses on building the coachee's ability to accomplish **specific tasks**, whereas the mentor has a wider perspective. The mentor typically has a **longer-term** relationship with the mentee, or is a counsellor on a **broader range of issues** at any given time.

There are a number of different mentoring roles you could find yourself playing – as an 'official' mentor if your organisation has a system for helping recently hired people, or as a longer-term, friendship-based mentor who counsels someone for a significant part of his or her career. Between these two extremes lies a variety of other types of relationship.

However, all mentoring roles use all or most of the seven types of assistance indicated opposite.

Seven Types of Mentoring Assistance

Type of assistance	How to do it
1. Helping the mentee to a positive mental attitude	See *Motivation,* pages 66 and 67
2. Listening when the mentee has a problem; identifying the mentee's feelings and legitimising them	Provide a 'listening ear', without a judgemental response. Explore options if appropriate
3. Providing appropriate information when needed	See *Providing Feedback*, pages 24 and 25. Mentors also provide access to privileged (but authorised) information
4. Encouraging exploration of options	See *GROW*, pages 30 and 31
5. Delegating tasks and authority	See *Skill/Will matrix*, pages 54 and 55
6. Effectively confronting negative behaviours	See *Providing Feedback*, pages 24 and 25
7. Providing a role model	Create opportunities for working together, where needed skills can be demonstrated and assimilated

Adapted from *Mentoring* by Gordon Shea

Exercise
- Review your performance as a mentor. Compare your perspectives with those of your mentee(s).

Before the sudden arrival of a coach and mentor, the young da Vinci felt that his job was somehow unfulfilling.

18. Reflecting on Coaching - a Summary

In which Alex recaps his thoughts on coaching

. . . Settling back into his poolside chair, and gazing out over the Aegean once again, Alex came to the end of his career 'flashback'. He reloaded the dictating machine which he had first picked up several hours earlier. 'Yes,' he thought, 'but what does the great coach *really* do, when we cut through all the frameworks?'

Pausing to collect his thoughts, he refilled his glass with ouzo, reapplied the Factor 6 sunscreen and began to speak into the machine again.

* * *

Let's take a working definition of coaching and then identify the skills and habits which characterise the effective coach. Most coaches have 'grooved' these coaching skills and habits into their daily lives.

Coaching aims to enhance the performance and learning ability of others. It involves providing feedback, but it also uses other techniques such as motivation, effective questioning and consciously matching your management style to each coachee's readiness to undertake a particular task. It is based on helping people to help themselves through interacting dynamically with them – it does not rely on a one-way flow of telling and instructing.

Figure 2 (next page) provides a structured list of the activities of the great coach in the workplace. Let's examine them in sequence.

1. *Setting the context.* This is a critical event; too often we dive into providing feedback with no warning. That can leave the coachee

Figure 2

The coachee's game plan

1. Set the context

   - Diagnose skill and will
   - Agree the approach
   - Build trust
   - Motivate

2. Provide ongoing coaching

   - Use GROW sessions (20-60 minutes)
   - Provide feedback (actionable, frequent, 5-10 minutes)
   - Give praise (frequent, where warranted, 1+ minutes)
   - Illustrate actively

3. Conclude effectively

   - Encourage coachee to reflect
   - Elicit feedback for coach
   - Agree next steps

---

feeling gratuitously 'judged' and unwilling to accept ideas which s/he might otherwise have taken on board.

So good coaches habitually make explicit with the coachee the context for their forthcoming interactions. (Figure 3 on the next page provides some examples.) However, the coach needs to do some homework first – particularly if s/he is the coachee's boss.

This includes:

- *Diagnosing the skill and will* of the coachee to accomplish the task. Refer back to the Skill/Will matrix on page 55.

- *Agreeing the approach to coaching.* The Skill/Will matrix will suggest the overall coaching approach you will want to take: Directing, Guiding, Exciting or Delegating (pages 55, 110 and 111). However, it is worth being explicit with the coachee about the logistics: How frequently will you provide feedback? What types of coaching sessions will you have? What preparation will you expect of the coachee? You should also make sure you know how your coachees prefer to take in information – by the written word (give them key points in writing), the spoken word (talk to them), visually (illustrate with charts and figures) or by doing (have them work with you in order to practise).

- *Building trust in the coaching relationship.* Effective coaching only really happens when the coachee trusts the coach. This trust may exist from previous interactions you have had with the coachee – or you may need to 'earn' it. A powerful way to do this is to disclose something of your own strengths, weaknesses and experiences. For example, you could share your last performance review with your coachee, or describe relevant situations you have confronted in the past.

- *Motivating the coachee.* Do you know what really motivates the people with whom you work? Try the following exercise: give your colleagues or team-mates a copy of pages 112 and 113, amended as you see fit, and share your – and the team's – completed results with them. You will be surprised at the wide variety of responses. Effective motivation requires two things.

Figure 3

Ways to make the context explicit

1. Obtaining coaching

    *   (To boss) 'I'm really trying to build my skills in [topic]. I'd be very grateful if you could coach me on this, during our next project. Would you be willing to do this? When would it be convenient to discuss the logistics of that coaching support?'

    *   (To peer) 'I've always thought you were really good at [topic]. I'm trying to get better at this myself. Could I seek your advice and coaching on this during the next few months? Perhaps we could meet for 30 minutes on Friday afternoons/over lunch/over a drink on the occasional evening?'

    *   (To more junior person) 'I'd really appreciate your feedback and suggestions on [topic]. Even if you think I'm good at this already, I'd appreciate your comments – please don't wait for me to ask.'

2. Providing coaching – see, particularly, Chapters 5 and 6

First, you must know what really excites your coachee about her/his job – why does s/he really come to work in the morning? Second, you will do well to paint an engaging vision of how well your coachee really could perform (Figure 4, next page), building the cycle of confidence explained on page 66.

2. *Providing ongoing guidance.* Once the context is understood and agreed, you're ready for a series of coaching interactions. You will already have agreed how often these discussions will take place and how long they will last. In practice, you are likely to use four types of interaction:

- *Substantive sessions of, say, 20 to 60 minutes based on the GROW structure* (refer back to page 30). If your coaching 'contract' extends over two to three months, you may decide to have three such sessions – at the beginning, middle and end of your collaboration. Try to vary the amount of time you spend on the Goals, Reality, Options and Wrap-up, to make the most effective use of your time with the coachee.

- *Brief discussions of five to ten minutes, to provide feedback in a timely manner,* soon after the coachee's actions which you have observed.

- *One minute (or longer) sessions of praise* – where warranted. Most coachees do not listen when the typical manager provides positive feedback. Why? Because the coachee is waiting for the inevitable 'but . . .' which normally follows, and which heralds a series of suggestions for improved performance. By sometimes providing unmitigated praise, you will find your coachee becoming more attentive to your comments and more trusting of you.

- *Active illustration* of how to accomplish the task at which the coachee is trying to build her/his skills. You can accomplish this by demonstration or by collaboration. For example, if you are helping the coachee to run meetings more effectively, you could demonstrate specific points by taking her/him along to one that you yourself are leading. Ask afterwards what s/he

Figure 4

Developing a vision

observed and what s/he might try differently next time (you could even ask for feedback on your own performance in running that meeting!).

Alternatively, you could collaborate – working with your coachee on a specific task. For example, if the coaching task is to analyse market research data with greater insight, you could work through the detailed data with your coachee so that s/he could see at first hand how insights can be generated.

You can obviously provide these *active* illustrations only if you yourself are relatively 'expert'. If you lack the necessary expertise in the area in question, you should suggest a 'role model' for the coachee to observe in action.

During these interactions, use the full repertoire of coaching tools which you now know about: the Ask/Tell spectrum (page 8), GROW (page 30), instant payoff coaching (page 49), pure feedback (page 24), motivation (page 66) and others.

3. *Concluding the coaching arrangement.* You will not want your coaching relationship to just 'fizzle out'. Exactly how you conclude it will depend on factors such as whether your coachee will, in any case, continue working with you or interacting with you socially. However, any conclusion should include at least three steps:

- *Reflection.* Reflection is a critical aspect of how most people learn (see *Educating the Reflective Practitioner* by Schon, cited in the Bibliography). Ensure that the coachee reviews and reflects upon what s/he has learned over the past few months.

- *Feedback to the **coach**.* Your coachee can probably give you some useful summary feedback on your coaching approach even if s/he has been doing so previously. Make sure you ask for it, and reflect on the experience yourself.

- *Next steps.* Decide whether this is 'goodbye' or 'au revoir'; or perhaps you have been coaching your partner at tennis, and it's time to swap roles.

* * *

Alex switched off the dictating machine, got up and stretched. He cast one more glance over the wine-dark sea and went indoors. He picked up the phone and called his secretary.

'I've been trying to get hold of you all afternoon,' she said, 'the Chairman would like a word with you.'

Five minutes later he put the phone down, just as his wife was coming in from the pool. 'Sarah, I've got some good news . . .'

The End

Appendices

Appendix 1

Coaching (Self-) Assessment Form

Answer the following questions for yourself and/or ask colleagues to complete a copy of this page based on their impressions of you.

How many times in the last week did I . . .

1.	Provide unconditional praise
2.	Give constructive feedback
3.	Check a colleague's level of motivation
4.	Inspire a colleague
5.	Ask for feedback
6.	Consciously delegate a task
7.	Hold a really effective team meeting
8.	Provide upward feedback
9.	Check a team's morale
10.	'Mentor' a more junior person

☐ Total

Totals

1 – 3 If you are not a recluse, you need to study and apply this book carefully

4 – 6 You can significantly increase your effectiveness at work by applying just a few tips from this book

7 – 8 You are nearly a master coach

9 – 10 Give this book to someone who needs it

Priority areas for me to work on

1.

2.

3.

Appendix 2

Feedback Plan

Three people to whom I could give useful feedback		
1.	2.	3.
Topics to cover		
Further information I need to gather		
When I will provide feedback		

Appendix 3

Examples of Useful Questions when Using 'GROW'

Goal

- What is it you would like to discuss?
- What would you like to achieve?
- What would you like from (to achieve in) this session?
- What would need to happen for you to walk away feeling that this time was well spent?
- If I could grant you a wish for this session, what would it be?
- What would you like to be different when you leave this session?
- What would you like to happen that is not happening now, or what would you like not to happen that is happening now?
- What outcome would you like from this session/discussion/ interaction?
- Is that realistic?
- Can we do that in the time we have available?
- Will that be of real value to you?

Reality

- What is happening at the moment?
- How do you know that this is accurate?
- When does this happen?
- How often does this happen? Be precise if possible.
- What effect does this have?
- How have you verified, or would you verify, that that is so?
- What other factors are relevant?
- Who else is relevant?
- What is their perception of the situation?
- What have you tried so far?

Options

- What could you do to change the situation?
- What alternatives are there to that approach?
- Tell me what possibilities for action you see. Do not worry about whether they are realistic at this stage.
- What approach/actions have you seen used, or used yourself, in similar circumstances?
- Who might be able to help?
- Would you like suggestions from me?
- Which options do you like the most?
- What are the benefits and pitfalls of these options?
- Which options are of interest to you?
- Rate from 1–10 your interest level in/the practicality of each of these options.
- Would you like to choose an option to act on?

Wrap-up

- What are the next steps?
- Precisely when will you take them?
- What might get in the way?
- Do you need to log the steps in your diary?
- What support do you need?
- How and when will you enlist that support?

Appendix 4

More Details on Applying the Skill/Will Matrix

Direct (skill and will are both low)
- First build the will
  - Provide clear briefing
  - Identify motivations
  - Develop a vision of future performance
- Then build the skill
  - Structure tasks for 'quick wins'
  - Coach and train
- Then sustain the will
  - Provide frequent feedback
  - Praise and nurture
- **BUT** supervise closely with tight control and clear rules/ deadlines

Guide (low skill, high will)
- Invest time early on
  - Coach and train
  - Answer questions/explain
- Create a risk-free environment to allow early 'mistakes'/ learning
- Relax control as progress is shown

Excite (high skill, low will)
- Identify reason for low will – e.g., task/management style/ personal factors
- Motivate (see Chapter 12)
- Monitor, feed back

Delegate (skill and will are both high)
- Provide freedom to do the job
  - Set objective, not method
  - Praise, don't ignore
- Encourage coachee to take responsibility
  - Involve in decision-making
  - Use 'You tell me what *you* think'
- Take appropriate risks
  - Give more stretching tasks
  - Don't over-manage

Appendix 5

Motivation Exercise – What Motivates You Most/Least

Have members of your team(s) complete copies of this page and share their results

Factor	Importance of factors*	Current satisfaction*
1. Manager showing concern for you as a person		
2. Having some authority		
3. Good personal relationships with manager		
4. Manager's decisiveness		
5. Examples provided by manager		
6. Being involved in planning your own work		
7. Recognition of your efforts		
8. Delegation of work to you		
9. Being promoted		
10. Customer/client contact		
11. Salary		
12. Extent to which you get on with your peers		
13. Praise		
14. Attaining your own goals and meeting targets		
15. Satisfaction with the job		
16. Working conditions		
17. Having responsibility for discrete areas of work		

* 1 = High, 4 = Low

Factor	Importance of factors*	Current satisfaction*
18. Working under pressure		
19. A competitive environment		
20. Your prospects of career development		
21. Constructive feedback and coaching		
22. Job security		
23. The result of the completed work		
24. Carrying out complex analysis		
25. The organisation's structure and processes		
26. Your personal job title		
27. Extent of supervision		
28. Social functions		
29. Detailed guidance on how to complete work tasks		
30. Working in a team		
31. Being given clear objectives		
32. Attending high-level meetings		
33. Starting work early in the morning		
34. Finishing work late in the evening		
35. Other (specify)		

* 1 = High, 4 = Low

Appendix 6

Team Performance Appraisal Form

Ask members of your team to complete and discuss copies of this form

Goal	Indicator	Current rating 1 = High, 4 = Low
Meaningful purpose	1. All team members feel a common and meaningful sense of purpose behind the project and are clear on its value	
Performance goals	2. The team is working towards achieving agreed goals in an effective manner	
Working approach	3. All team members contribute to the 'real work' on the project, and have a definite and positive role to play 4. All team members provide each other with satisfactory real-time feedback 5. The team operates in a non-hierarchical manner (i.e., team members feel that their contributions are fully heard and appraised)	
Complementary skills	6. The team has accessed the right mix of skills, directly and indirectly	
Mutual accountability	7. All team members feel that the achievement of the team goals is recognised and regarded above individual contributions 8. Team members provide mutual support and encouragement. Each team member feels accountable for the team's success 9. The team is providing opportunities and support to individuals in meeting their goals	
Overall	10. The team has maintained a high level of morale 11. All team members have felt strongly motivated throughout this project	

Suggestions for improvement

Bibliography

COACHING

| Blanchard, K & S Johnson | *The One Minute Manager* | HarperCollins, London, 1983 |

Quick and easy introduction to the basics of coaching and feedback

---

| Bone, D | *Practical Guide to Effective Listening* | Kogan Page, London, 1991 |

A short, comprehensive guide to skills in listening

| Buckley, R & J Caple | *One-to-one Training & Coaching Skills* | Kogan Page, London, 1991 |

A concise guide to coaching in the business environment

| Clutterbuck, D | *Everyone Needs a Mentor* | Institute of Personnel Management, London, 1991 |

Helpful guide to thinking through the implications of coaching (mentoring) within your own organisation

---

| Evered, R & J Selman | Coaching & the Art of Management | *Organisational Dynamics* 18 2: 16 – 32, 1989 |

Short background article on the role of the coach

Gallway, T	*The Inner Game of Golf*	Jonathan Cape, London, 1975
Gallway, T	*The Inner Game of Tennis*	Jonathan Cape, London, 1975
Gallway, T & B Kriegel	*Inner Skiing*	Jonathan Cape, London, 1975

Introductions to 'coachee-centred' philosophy, principles and questioning techniques using sport

---

| Megginson, D & T Baydell | *A Manager's Guide to Coaching* | British Association for Commercial & Industrial Education, London, 1979 |

A short book about coaching

COACHING – continued

| Mink, O,
KQ Owen &
BP Mink | *Developing High
Performance People:
The Art of Coaching* | Addison-Wesley Publishing
Company, Reading,
Massachusetts, 1993 |

Detailed and painstaking description of coaching and its various applications and techniques

| Parsloe, E | *Coaching, Mentoring
and Assessing: A Practical
Guide to Developing
Competence* | Kogan Page, London, 1992 |

A useful reference for those involved in coaching

| Shea, GF | *Mentoring* | Kogan Page, London, 1992 |

Guide to using mentoring as a tool for empowerment

| Whitmore, J | *Coaching for Performance:
A Practical Guide to
Growing Your Own Skills* | Nicholas Brealey, London,
1994 |

Excellent 'self-help' guide for the development of coaching skills

PYSCHOLOGY AND COUNSELLING

| Board, R de | *Counselling Skills* | Wildwood House, London,
1987 |

Down-to-earth guide on counselling, for the manager

| Garfield, C | *Peak Performance* | Warner Books, New York,
1984 |

Helpful background from sports psychologists about the impact of mental state on performance

| Gibb, JR | *Trust: A New View of Personal & Organisational Development* | Guild of Tutors Press, Los Angeles, 1978 |

One of the earliest advocates of Group Development in organisations

| Harris, T | *I'm OK, You're OK: A Practical Guide to Transactional Analysis* | Harper & Row, New York, 1969 |

Outstanding primer on Transactional Analysis, but not as simple as it first appears

| Keirsey, D & M Bates | *Please Understand Me: Character & Temperament Types* | Prometheus Nemesis Book Company, Del Mar, California, 1984 |

Introduction to the Myers-Briggs Framework

| Whitmore, D | *Psychosynthesis Counselling in Action* | Sage Publications Limited, London, 1991 |

Techniques and examples of Dr Robert Assagioli's psychosynthesis

LEARNING

| Argyris, C | *Overcoming Organisational Defences: Facilitating Organisational Learning* | Allyn & Bacon, Sydney, 1990 |

Thorough analysis of how social norms and learned behaviour can have counter-productive impact on learning and communication

| Brookfield, S | *Understanding and Facilitating Adult Learning* | Jossey-Bass Publishers, San Franscisco, 1991 |

Introduction to the special challenges in helping adults learn new things

GENERAL

Bandler, R & J Grindler	*Frogs into Princes*	Real People Press, Moab, Utah, 1979

Good introduction to the principles of Neuro Linguistic Programming, as applied in daily life

Bennis, W	*On Becoming a Leader*	Addison-Wesley Publishing Company, Reading, Massachusetts,1989

An insightful book by a pioneering leader and behavioural scientist

Covey, SR	*The Seven Habits of Highly Effective People*	Simon & Schuster, London, 1992

A highly effective bestseller on how to be more effective

Hersey, P & K Blanchard	*Situational Leadership: A Summary*	University Associates, San Diego, California, 1982

One view of management development which has had significant impact

Hofstede, G	*Cultures and Organisations*	HarperCollins, London, 1991

Implications of cultures on how we manage and interact

Katzenbach, J & D Smith	*The Wisdom of Teams*	HarperCollins, New York, 1991

Advice on the art of building teams and teamwork for high performance

Schon, D	*Educating the Reflective Practitioner*	Jossey-Bass Publishers, San Francisco, 1987

How reflecting on experience can help professionals to learn

Glossary

AID – see *Feedback*

Blocks to coaching – A reluctance to coach in certain situations, for reasons which are often misguided. For example the 'control freak' often claims that s/he never has enough time to invest in coaching. This person rarely delegates and becomes caught in a vicious circle of workaholism. There are ways out of these and other predicaments.

Coaching – Coaching aims to enhance the performance and learning ability of others. It involves providing feedback, but it also uses other techniques such as motivation, effective questioning and consciously matching your management style to the coachee's readiness to undertake a particular task. It is based on helping the coachee to help her/himself through interacting dynamically with her/him – it does not rely on a one-way flow of telling and instructing.

Delegate (as a management style: see *Skill/Will matrix*) – The preferred approach to managing and coaching people who have high skill and high will to complete the specific task at hand.

Direct (as a management style: see *Skill/Will matrix*) – The preferred approach to managing and coaching people who have low skill and low will to complete the specific task at hand.

Excite (as a management style: see *Skill/Will matrix*) – The preferred approach to managing and coaching people who have high skill but low will to complete the specific task at hand.

Feedback – The process of highlighting to the coachee (a) recent actions, (b) the impact of these actions, and (c), in the broader meaning of the term, desired alternative outcomes where appropriate. Use the acronym *AID* to remember the three steps (**A**ction, **I**mpact, **D**esired alternative outcomes).

Goals (a step within *GROW*) – The objectives of the specific coaching session, within the context of the coachee's longer-term development objectives.

GROW – A four-step structure which helps the coach and coachee to move effectively through a coaching session: **G**oals, **R**eality, **O**ptions, **W**rap-up:
- The coach typically uses both 'ask' and 'tell' within each step of the process.
- Clearly, the coach needs to iterate flexibly between the four steps when this is called for.

Guide (as a management style: see *Skill/Will matrix*) – The preferred approach to managing and coaching people who have low skill and high will to complete the specific task at hand.

Instant payoff coaching – A technique for helping someone to resolve a problem in a limited period of time – e.g., 10–15 minutes. The technique focuses on first envisioning what the successful outcome would look or feel like. Subsequent discussion focuses on identifying the source of constraints or blocks to effective action, and how to deal with them.

Mentoring – A role which includes coaching, but also embraces broader counselling and support, such as career counselling, privileged access to information, etc.

Motivation – A critical aspect of managing and coaching – with motivational factors differing widely from individual to individual.

Options (a step within *GROW*) – The brainstormed list of ways in which the coachee can improve her/his performance in a specific area.

Reality (a step within *GROW*) – A description from either the coach – or the coachee her/himself – of what the coachee has done effectively or ineffectively in a recent situation.

Skill/Will matrix – A simple way to identify the coach's or manager's appropriate management style, based on the skill and will of the coachee to complete the specific task in question. The four resulting management styles are *Direct, Excite, Guide and Delegate.*

Tao (pronounced 'how' with an initial 'd') – Taoism is a practical philosophy of life which was first codified in China over 2,000 years ago. It
maintains that everything is influenced – directly or indirectly – by
everything else; that apparent opposites are merely differing manifes-
tations of an underlying unity; and that change is caused by the continuous interplay between yin and yang, as suggested by the familiar
symbol ◉ . The word 'Tao' means 'the way', in the sense of 'the way
in which things happen'.

In terms of coaching, Tao means 'the way in which I work and live in
order to derive energy from interacting dynamically with people and
things as opposed to expending energy by continually "going against
the grain"'.

If yin is 'building the skills and abilities of those who work with us',
then yang is 'becoming more effective by delegating to those people
whom we have helped to become more able'.

Wrap-up (a step within *GROW*) – The coachee's next steps after the coaching session. The plan should be specific, achievable within the agreed
timescale, and reflect any assistance needed from third parties.

Acknowledgements

This book grew out of a coaching programme launched throughout McKinsey & Company in the UK during 1990. A previous internal version of this guide – written for that programme – therefore benefited from significant input from many of my colleagues across the firm – particularly Sandra Charalambous, Humphrey Cobbold, Kate Grussing, Andrew Glover, Judith Hazlewood, Julian Seaward, Frazer Smith, Kathryn Thomas and Jim Wendler.

Norman Sanson, the firm's UK Managing Director, deserves special acknowledgement. He not only had the vision to launch that initial coaching programme, but also contributed to this book through personal example. I am also indebted to my other partners around the globe for their support.

Ben Cannon is a Director of Alexander – the consultancy firm which helps organisations to build effectiveness and improve the performance of key individuals, teams or even the whole work force, through coaching. The firm has successfully coached the author and his colleagues, and Ben helped bring the book alive, contributing to a number of chapters.

Peter Bamford, Managing Director (Retail) of WH Smith, kindly read through the manuscript and suggested improvements based on his extensive business experience.

I should also like to thank the McKinsey & Company team responsible for the completion of this book: Partha Bose (Director of Communications–Europe) provided both incisive comment and strong personal encouragement. Robert Whiting (Publications Editor) and Deborah Thomas (Editor) added continuity to the story and removed anachronism and zeugma. Carole Gardner, Alison Mills and Steph Saul creatively enhanced the book's format.

Finally, I thank HIGGINS (whose cartoons still make me laugh on the twentieth re-reading), and Martin Liu, Lucinda McNeile and Juliet Van Oss (my editors at HarperCollins) who shepherded this book through unexpected turns with the greatest of professionalism, and who provided their feedback to the author in the manner of great coaches.

Index